The
Heart
of the MATTER

Previous Works by Paul Loeb

Paul Loeb's Complete Book of Dog Training
You Can Train Your Cat
Supertraining Your Dog
Cathletics
Nutrition and Your Dog
Smarter Than You Think

The Heart
of the MATTER

Breaking Codes and Making Connections
Between You and Your Dog or Your Cat

Paul Loeb & Suzanne Hlavacek

POCKET BOOKS
New York London Toronto Sydney Tokyo Singapore

POCKET BOOKS, a division of Simon & Schuster Inc.
1230 Avenue of the Americas, New York, NY 10020

Library of Congress Cataloging-in-Publication Data

Loeb, Paul, 1935–
    The heart of the matter : breaking codes and making connections
between you and your dog or cat / Paul Loeb & Suzanne Hlavacek.
        p.   cm.
    ISBN 0-671-02790-5
    1. Dogs—Behavior.   2. Cats—Behavior.   3. Dogs—Training.
4. Cats—Training.   5. Human–animal relationships.   I. Hlavacek,
Suzanne.   II. Title.
SF433.L64   1999
636.5′0896203—dc21   99-26926
                                                      CIP

First Pocket Books hardcover printing July 1999

10   9   8   7   6   5   4   3   2   1

POCKET and colophon are registered trademarks of
Simon & Schuster Inc.

Printed in the U.S.A.

For John and Pegge Hlavacek,
a couple of first-class world travelers.

For Willy and Tibby.

ACKNOWLEDGMENTS

To:

Tristram Coburn, our editor.
Amy Rogers, in publicity.
Al Zuckerman, our agent.
A "high maintenance" thank-you.

CONTENTS

CONTENTS

CONTENTS

CHAPTER 1

Soul Mirror

Probably one of our more interesting and surprising cases surfaced in the Flatbush Avenue section of Brooklyn. The man in this case was a Romanian Gypsy, a certified, card-carrying psychic, who's handle was one Peretz Mendel Zigenlaub.

He contacted us because he had a major problem with Ouspenskaya, his dog. She was a thief. Not your petty kind of thief, this dog was a vision thief. A one-of-a-kind thief of the mind. She had stolen his visions, visions and secrets handed down to him by his ancestors, over hundreds of years, from Zigenlaub to Zigenlaub. This dog had stolen Zigenlaub's ability to delve into the past and to see into the future. And this Zigenlaub, a veil baby born, had been assured at birth of these special powers by the ancients. It had always been said that babies born in this manner, covered with a veil, would always have these special powers of perception and good fortune. Now they were gone, these powers. Stolen by a dog.

What had thoroughly baffled this man, what had bent him out of shape, what had shaken him to the very core of his Gypsy soul, was HOW? How could this dog, or any dog, get into someone's mind and steal visions? How could he get them back? This was far beyond Zigenlaub and far beyond comprehension. It was entering the realm of the bizarre.

If a dog takes a shoe, a book, something real, something solid, something you can put your hands on, you put your hands on it and take it back. You take it out of the dog's mouth, and that's it, it's over with. How in the world can you make a dog drop a dream? How can you make a dog give that dream back to you?

This theft, the hand-me-down-visions caper, had left Zigenlaub with nothing but an empty head. A shell that had once held the Zigenlaub family vision secrets, the all-seeing powers of the ages. Now the gift was held in the hands—no, the paws—of a dog, a mixer from Flatbush Avenue.

Zigenlaub, now an empty mind, totally devoid of visions, dreams, and thoughts, was a mindless, rudderless ship at sea.

At sea, all he could see in the dark sky was his dog's smiling face. This face was the only star he had to plot a course by, to put his trust in. But to trust a thief? This face in the sky, this Ouspenskaya face, was a constellation of floppy ears, happy, bright eyes, and a shiny, wet, purple nose. In her mouth, she held a small, brown paper bag. This bag held the purloined visions, the stolen, Zigenlaub, centuries-old family jewels.

Zigenlaub was totally helpless. On his rudderless ship he could be dashed and smashed against life's rocky road. He feared the end of the Zigenlaub vision line was near. And all because of a Gypsy dog named Ouspenskaya, she, the cunning vision thief.

This was a riddle he couldn't solve. Zigenlaub was in a catch-22. He needed to solve this riddle, and soon. But he couldn't. He needed to see the answer. But he had no vision. And if you have no vision, you can't see. And if you can't see, you can't solve any riddles. How would Zigenlaub, a man with no vision, rudderless, ever find his way home again?

And what home was there for this visionless man to come home to?

Well, there was his Ouspenskaya, the vision thief. Having successfully gotten away with his mind, she now had taken control of the rest of Zigenlaub's world.

She was running his life. She was reshuffling his fortune cards, playing hide-n-seek with his crystal ball, and tearing up his talisman bag, flinging the charms to the four winds, so that Zigenlaub hardly knew where he was at anymore or which way was up or down. He had no idea of anything what with the past, the present, and the future being all mixed up and hanging in the balance of an Ouspenskaya raid. Zigenlaub was frightened that he might read someone their past, what was really in their future.

If Ouspenskaya didn't like a client, she might growl at them or even bite them. But for sure, she would intimidate and control all of them. What most of his clients really feared, what put knots in the pits of their stomachs, was that she, Ouspenskaya, might cast a spell on them, since she now held the Zigenlaub hand-me-down visions and secrets.

In order to make her happy and keep her aggressive tendencies from erupting, to make sure Ouspenskaya never lost patience with them, they brought her many gifts. Not diamonds, not gold nor silver; she wasn't impressed by inanimate objects that had no alluring smell to activate her powers. She turned up her nose at these useless things. The clients found the best offerings came from caring kitchens. Strawberry shortcake got you to the head of the line.

But spells or no, and loaded with bags of good food, they kept coming back. All were drawn in by the seductive, overpowering thrill of fear, fear of the unknown, all were drawn in by the possibility of finding the answers to a richer, fuller life. All were drawn to consult with Ouspenskaya, the all-powerful one, the oracle, she, the mixer from Flatbush Avenue, Brooklyn.

What really bothered Zigenlaub, what really blew through his empty mind, besides a draft, was that he had lost all of his clients, they only wanted to see Ouspenskaya. Not him. They felt she could give them the answers they were seeking. Not him. They came to see her, this healer. Not him. They came to see the future, they came to see the past, they came to see inside themselves. They came to be put on the right path in life. Zigenlaub couldn't do it anymore. He hadn't any mind to do it with, anymore.

This whole reversal of fortune was making Zigenlaub crazy, giving him major migraine-type headaches, lower-back pain, and spasms that would continue around the clock. This man's pain was not to be believed. All because of this Ouspenskaya, this mysterious minx, of many mixed origins, who showed no mercy, no signs of letting up on our Peretz Mendel Zigenlaub.

Peretz was lying on the floor on his back—that's how we found him when we arrived in Flatbush. His dog asked us if we wanted something to drink, since it was such a hot day. We said yes and thanked her.

We spent several hours with Peretz and Ouspenskaya. We wanted to patch things up between the two of them. Peretz was afraid to talk. He was afraid to say anything. He was afraid to contradict Ouspenskaya in any way—maybe she wouldn't give back his visions ever again if he did. And he was afraid to get up because his back was killing him.

It was clear to us that all Ouspenskaya ever wanted was good food, good friendship, and most of all she wanted him, Peretz Mendel Zigenlaub to know and understand her. After all she was very sensitive and tired of living with someone so selfish, so self-centered, and so insensitive. He didn't deserve to be a psychic. Let alone a hand-me-down one. He couldn't even see what she needed. So, how could this visionless man ever think that he could help anyone else, besides himself?

The vision theft had been a last-ditch effort to get his attention, and to get him to listen. Peretz promised to change for the better. Ouspenskaya agreed to give him back his mind, if he kept his promise. If he didn't, she was going to take it, and this time Peretz Mendel Zigenlaub's mind would be gone in a flush.

But she felt he should be weaned from no mind, slowly, to a full mind. She was afraid to give him too much of his mind all at once—he might get sick and have diarrhea. You know, they say, that sudden changes in food, even food for the mind, can do this.

The cut communication line seemed to have been spliced back together. This time tied in a herculean knot, for strength and good luck.

We were leaving when suddenly Peretz Zigenlaub, from the floor, gave a deep sigh of relief, as if a giant burden had been lifted off him. He fell into a deep sleep. A voice came out of the deep-sleeping Peretz Zigenlaub and told us we had better sit down and listen. We couldn't argue with this voice, it was everywhere and yet nowhere. So, we sat, and we listened.

The voice started to take on a shape. As the shape materialized, it took on a purple hue, and the form of a dog. A dog, a beautiful dog, one that looked somewhat similar to deep-sleeping Peretz, but better looking.

This dog then jumped right out of the sleeping psychic and ran immediately into the kitchen for some good food. A large pot of homemade goulash happened to be simmering on the stove. The delicious smell of this spicy goulash was probably what had drawn him out. Evidently, he was hungry and wanted to eat. Good food has drawing value.

Ouspenskaya was happy to see the purple dog, a dog she knew well. The dog's name was Plum. She had always had a soft spot for this Plum.

Purple Plum, now stuffed full of goulash, burped and got ready to speak. We couldn't move; some invisible, strong, and yet gentle force was holding us fast in our seats. Plum delivered his state-of-the-heart message.

He wanted to let us know that we all have an animal spirit inside to guide us. It's just that we've forgotten how to trust our spirits.

Plum explained it matter-of-factly:

"People say their eyes are the mirror of the soul. That's true enough, as far as it goes. But how far can these eyes see? Eyes are subjective and speculative. They lie and they can be fooled. You look in a mirror, you see yourself, and that is all you can see. You check to see if you are groomed well enough to face the world. Or, do you need to add or take something away? People eyes lie, about themselves, and about you.

"But if you want to know what you really look like, who you are, if you want to see beyond the surface of the glass, if you dare to look at the real you, then you will most certainly want to consult with the Soul Mirror. The best Soul Mirrors we know are us animals that live with you, your cats, your dogs, and others.

"They'll let you know the truth in the blink of an eye. You can't lie to a Soul Mirror. Their powers of perception are absolute, and awesome. On top of that, and whether you like it or not, your Soul Mirror is one with you always. Try to get one out of your mind. Impossible!

"Now on the other hand, let's look at a simple possession, a pet. A pet is put away with all the other toys at the end of the day, or when you are gone, 'it' is locked up in a box, a garage, or a small room. A pet's only function is to be a toy or a thing.

A pet has no importance in your life beyond 'its' ability to amuse and entertain.

"But watch out for the Soul Mirror! When he's around, you're in the presence of a powerhouse, one unequaled. So get out of the way. Give this powerhouse room to be.

"The ground shakes, the heavens roar, the wind blows, and all the gods smile down and follow the Soul Mirror. With the biggest heart, the wettest nose, this compassionate, mighty spirit is the pathfinder par excellence. Through your Soul Mirror you can find your way home. An omnipotent genie who lives not in a bottle but in your heart and mind. And if you're nice to him, you will get back much more than what you gave.

"How will you communicate with the Soul Mirror? Will you tell him, 'Sit'? Will you lock him up in a cage? Will you deny him your food? Or, will you keep him happy and comfortable?

"He's the only one who will never, ever lie to you and will accept you, warts and all. Are you going to throw this gift away? Do you think you'll find a more loyal friend?

"By the way, you don't own a Soul Mirror; if you're lucky, a Soul Mirror will share his valuable time and self with you.

"The Soul Mirror has the aspect of the sphinx. He is inscrutable in his deepest thoughts and inner being, like a Buddha. He reserves judgment on your shortcomings, accepts your limitations; he is at one with his universe and keeps his true counsel and wisdom with the gods, the spirit worlds, and Mother Nature, those who truly can hear him and who allow the Soul Mirror his true and full expression.

"He sends out a strong life force in an attempt to lift you higher than you are, to lift you to a level you cannot reach or find or get to or even see exists, without him. These swift couriers will guide and light the way; you just need to be willing to follow with a compass set on this true star.

"Eyes are the mirror of the soul? That's a lot of horse pucky.

7

What a joke. That lying eyes can mirror the soul? Who are you kidding?

"Soul Mirrors, no matter their power—no matter their omniscient gifts and happy presence—Soul Mirrors can break. Be careful when polishing these mirrors so you don't lose your soul."

We had questions for Plum, but he took none. He was finished. This silver-tongued orator turned and morphed back into Zigenlaub, who slowly came to with a smile on his face, a knowing smile. He seemed to have finally solved the riddles and gotten back his visions, visions that had been fleeting, confusing, and elusive, sometimes even a little frightening. Now all the fragments had come back together to give him a complete image. He did feel slightly nauseous though. Must have been all the visions coming back at once.

On the way out, Ouspenskaya handed us one of Zigenlaub's cards, with a 20 percent discount for a next reading of the future. Then she turned to Zigenlaub and said, "Mend your ways, Mendel."

CHAPTER 2

The List

Dogs and Cats. They bite. You're told it's only "nipping" and "mouthing." They fight. You're told, "Boys will be boys." They are destructive. You're told, "They're teething." They are barking, chewing, pissing, scratching, jumping. You're told they have a classic case of acute separation anxiety, and the ultimate treatment, you're told, is habit-forming drugs.

They are locked up in solitary confinement, imprisoned in a cage or crate, and you're led to believe that these cages and crates are condos and your dogs, these "cave" animals, love to live in them. They wear choke collars that choke and you're led to believe they don't choke. They wear prong or pinch collars that put holes in their necks, that hurt like hell, and you're led to believe they're harmless and painless. They are fed bad food and you're told it's the best and only food for them and they shouldn't eat anything else, or they might get sick and die.

Step back from all of this double-talk that you have been

spooned and think about it. It strikes us as tall tales, "told by an idiot, full of sound and fury, signifying nothing." Thanks, Shakespeare.

All of the above contraptions do hurt, both the mind and the body of your best friends.

In *The Heart of the Matter*, we are featuring case histories and stories, further adventures with our proven Magic Touch Communication system. This thinking person's information filter will remove all the confusing stuff and nonsense that obfuscates the issues of the health, well-being, and behavior of your dog or cat. Sometimes it seems the more intelligent people are, the quicker they lose their common sense in matters relating to their dog and cat. And no wonder, when all the information has been skewed, mixed up, controlled, and manipulated.

Let's get back the common sense that has been lost along the way, let's get back in touch with reality. Call a spade a spade, if that's what it is, don't call it a ham sandwich. You need the right tools for the job at hand; you cannot dig a ditch with a ham sandwich, you'll need that spade.

Get some real answers to real problems, real fast! From the simple and common dilemmas to the most difficult and complex ones, you will find clearly defined techniques and easy, practical solutions. Sound too good to be true? Wait, there's more. You will get your life back because there are no tedious, time-consuming, boring practice sessions that go on forever.

Your dog's and cat's natural abilities, intelligence, and super-senses are respected and brought into play, to teach you to teach them how to be well-behaved, truly integrated family members and trusted friends.

Learn about nutrition and how the right kind of food will help you shape the behavior and well-being of your dog and cat. You can solve a multitude of health problems just by making a few simple dietary changes. Diet, a crucial component of your animal's life, usually neglected and overlooked, should not be dominated by commercial pet-food companies and veterinarians. It's time for you to take the reins and be well informed about alternatives.

Learn how to stop aggression in all of its forms—the gamut from such simple annoying headaches as whining, pissing, chewing, pulling, jumping, and barking to the most downright dangerous migraines of biting, fighting, attacking, and even killing.

If any of the following relates to you, your dog, or your cat, you'll need our oak-handled, titanium spade to uncover powerful alternatives to standard limited practices that have all been defined and stockpiled, hidden and buried, deep under the umbrella term of "training."

The List

Are you allergic to your dog or cat?

Does your dog or cat suffer from a multitude of allergies and skin problems?

Is your dog or cat becoming a drug addict? Loaded with steroids, Valium, Prozac, or other assorted drug therapies?

Are you tired of spending more time at your veterinarian's office than at home?

Do you think a choke collar or a pinch collar really doesn't choke, pinch, or poke holes in your dog?

Do you keep your dog locked up in a cage or a crate? Are you aware of the insidious side effects of this inhumane solitary confinement?

Is your dog or cat aggressive toward people or other animals?

Is your dog a big-time barker?

Is your dog or cat destructive?

Is your dog or cat out of control?

Do you find there is never enough time in a day to practice your dog lessons, and no matter how much time you practice, your dog still doesn't listen to you?

Do you think your dog's or your cat's problems might be psychological?

Do you think your dog or cat could be suffering from acute separation anxiety or any other fears and phobias?

Do you think your dog or cat is just too stupid to learn?

Do you know how your dog's or cat's emotions relate to his abilities to learn?

Do you find that after a few days the "experts'" solutions have failed you?

Do you get tired of the "kiss the puppy or kitty expert" who gives you no help?

Do you blame yourself for failing your dog or your cat?

Do you blame your dog or your cat for failing you?

Do you get depressed, tired, angry, frustrated, and are you getting ready to give up?

Do you know what the best food is for your dog and cat?

Do you know that the wrong diet can be detrimental not only to a dog's or cat's health but also to his behavior and learning abilities?

Do you think commercial food companies and veterinarians should have the last word on your dog's or cat's nutrition, health, and behavior?

Do you think you should listen to the promises of major food companies for your own health and nutrition?

How many sources are available to you regarding your health and well-being? How many sources are available for your dog or cat?

Does your dog or cat need to lose weight?
How much exercise does your dog or cat really need?

Get your life back on line posthaste. All of the above can be solved either immediately or within a short time ... permanently! Without unnecessary medication, gimmicks, restraining devices, or "training" with its list of excuses and its impossible, unrealistic practice time.

Think about this. You get yourself a dog or a cat. You bring him home. You hug him and kiss him and tell him how much you love him. And then you won't let him eat what you eat, and as for the dog, you make him live in a solitary-confinement crate or cage. We don't think that's love. Love is sharing full-time. If you want to keep your dog in a crate or a cage, you might as well keep the dog's cage next to the birdcage or the fish tank, or on a shelf with your other toys and possessions.

You will learn an entirely new philosophy and a different way, in *every* which way, how to live with, love, and understand your furry, four-footed friends, and they will learn all about you and still love and accept you, even with all of your excess baggage.

You can transform that seemingly impossible dog or cat into a perfect one and have a good time at the same time. And your dog or cat will do you a good turn in return and transform you from an impossible person into a possible one.

Now begins the journey into the Soul Mirror, where there's more to see than what meets the eye.

CHAPTER 3

Heart of the Matter

Pickett's Charge

Wednesday, July 1, 1998

We got a call from Gettysburg, Pennsylvania. It seemed that Pickett was charging again. Not the General Pickett from Lee's Confederate army, but Pickett, the powerful three-and-a-half-pound Yorkie, and this Pickett, this little Pickett, was gaining ground.

Thursday, July 2, 1998

Pickett was getting worse. He was out of control and charging at everyone and everything in the house. Pickett charged the phone when it rang and anyone who answered it. When the doorbell sounded, it alerted Pickett for battle. He would charge the door and anyone who tried to enter thereby. When no doorbell or phone was ringing, Pickett would charge the hands that fed him, and the feet that belonged to the hands that fed him. And any other part of the feeder's body he could reach.

Pickett, this ten-inch-long, people-seeking missile, would skillfully charge anyone who happened to be innocently sitting on the couch and unaware of his love for these devastating, explosive, surprise attacks. The attacks were fast and furious, especially if food was being served, and double especially if it was Pickett's favorite food, anything in the realm of rich, whipped, creamy desserts. He would charge, and these innocent victims would hastily and chaotically retreat to the bathroom, the bedroom, or to any room with a strong, solid, defensive door that could be closed and locked . . . fast. It was clear. Pickett had to be stopped.

Friday, July 3, 1998

But Pickett miscalculated and made a grave error the day he charged General Lee. Lee, a large, majestic, white-bearded, gray cat, had his own battle plan, and he was the only one who knew how to deal with this Pickett. Lee grinned like a Cheshire cat when he successfully repulsed Pickett on one of his famous rampaging charges. This skirmish happened in the morning, in the kitchen, near the food, while Lee was trying to eat his breakfast of French toast. We believe that it was the intoxicating mixture of the French toast, maple syrup, and butter that attracted Pickett's interest. He came, this master of the charge, he saw, he readied to conquer, for the toast he smelled.

The general stood his ground, patiently biding his time. He watched as Pickett positioned himself for this patented charge. Waited, his body and tail starting to expand and puff. Pickett charged. Lee, with the speed of light, hit him, not once but twice, boxing his ears, stopping Pickett in his tracks and sending him reeling and rolling away, with a bloody nose and his tail between his legs. We estimate the whole battle took no more than four seconds, and Lee, turning around as if nothing had happened, dug into his morning meal with gusto. Pickett stopped charging Lee right then and there, permanently.

Saturday, July 4, 1998, Independence Day

General Lee celebrated this Fourth of July. His magic touch had stopped Pickett from charging and being a total pain in the neck. His technique had worked immediately, permanently, and without having to be practiced. Lee's technique proved effective when the target happened to be within paw's reach.

Fionnula and Beau, who live with this dynamic duo, celebrated this Fourth of July with fireworks, a barbecue, and by acquiring all the necessary and pertinent information to stop Pickett's charging as fast as the general did. They became experts in the use of our Magic Touch.

The Magic Touch, one of the three key elements of our program, has no boundaries. You are limited only by your aim, your eye-hand coordination, and your willingness to solve the problem.

Once Pickett learned not to bother the general, especially when he was having his breakfast, they became good friends with a mutual respect for each other. Would you say Lee had *trained* Pickett? Or rather, that this lightning-fast southpaw had *taught* Pickett a lesson? The general didn't train, he taught. We don't train, we teach. This book doesn't train, it teaches.

Many books have been written about the proper care in the bringing up and teaching of children, and we're sure there will be many more on the subject. But none of them are thought of as "training" books. Why not? They are books that teach parents how to bring up their children in one way or another.

Why aren't they considered "training" books? If they were considered "training" books, then they would be limited psychologically and in practical, usable information, life's lessons and subtleties. What do we mean by this?

If a parent wanted to "train" their child to do a specific task such as sail a boat, ride a bike, tie a shoelace, then they might pick up a "training" manual to learn these specific how-tos. But if a parent wants help in all areas of raising their child such as in language development, emotional guidance and understanding, proper nutrition, and why children do what they do and at what ages they do certain things, then they would want a book that gives them insightful, complete, holistic, and comprehensive information. Furthermore, parents might even feel insulted at the prospect of having to "train" their child with the help of a child "training" manual.

Although there are obvious differences between cats, dogs, and children, they all still have to be brought up properly and taught how to fit into your life. All of these responsibilities, and they are responsibilities, are far more demanding and a far cry from the limitations of just plain "no, bad, sit, stay, heel" archaic training.

Just as books on how to raise a child contain some behavior modification, they are still not referred to as child "training" books, and just as there is some behavior modification in our books, they are still not "training" books.

To begin with, because words have power and meaning, it is necessary to institute a mind shift, a way to break the patterning control of the word *training*. This is necessary to get you out of that small box, that limited, restrictive way of thinking that will eventually lead nowhere.

You have to open yourself up to a new thought process and understand that teaching your dogs and cats, bringing them up and raising them properly, involves much more than just "training." Just by using the word *training* you are limiting your dogs' and cats' learning capabilities as well as yours. It will bring you all down to a lower level, with the lowest of expectations.

This Is Not a Training Book

If this sounds like semantical hairsplitting, consider this. In William Safire's column "On Language" in the *New York Times Magazine* (January 25, 1998) he wrote about Wandering Words. "Barnacles attach themselves to words, as crustaceans to ships' hulls, freighting a term with meaning beyond the ship itself." We do not want to be burdened by barnacles on our ship. *Training*, when used with the subject of dogs and cats, has become so loaded with barnacles that the whole ship is in danger of going out of control and sinking. We want to unburden ourselves of the doctrines and dogmas of "dog obedience training."

Keep in mind that thinking about teaching as opposed to "training" is more than just a mind shift creating a new paradigm. When you go into "training," you also have a physical dimension associated with the term. You will carry along a lot of unnecessary, and often harmful, baggage onto that sinking ship. What are these barnacles, doctrines, and dogmas?

Barnacles, Doctrines, and Dogmas

First: Training behavior. Practice and repetitive direction. You take a course in a private or group obedience class and hope for the best. We have no argument with that. However, the "no, sit, stay, heel" training you are taught will be useless if your dog is biting, barking, peeing all over your house, or just not listening to you. These "no, sit, stay, heel" words, either used singly or in any combination, are the remedies you will be left with to control all of your dog's unacceptable behavior. The more they don't work, the more you are told to practice them. It becomes a never ending chore, because no matter how much you practice, it will never be enough and it will never work.

Second: Training stuff. Cage and crate confinement. This lockup will permanently prevent the natural and normal bonding between you and your dog. Your dog will for sure bond to the crate or cage and not to you.

More stuff. All paraphernalia, such as muzzles, choke collars, prong collars, electric collars, electric invisible fences, and other restrictive devices, will restrict your dog from learning any kind of constructive behavior from you. Your dog is being controlled only by these restraints and devices, but not by you on any level whatsoever.

If a human being were restrained with a choke or prong collar, and then locked in solitary confinement, would you expect that person to be a happy camper and well balanced after all of that torture? We don't think so. When conventional stuff doesn't work, you will then be taken to the higher-end stuff, high-as-a-kite end stuff such as Prozac, Valium, and other tranquilizers and mood- and mind-altering drugs to control your dog's behavior and in this case even your cat's.

People who are given these drugs must be and are supervised by doctors. The doctors will ask them questions about the effects of the drugs, how they are working, if there are side effects. Monitoring will be constant. How do you ask your dog or cat any of these questions? How can they possibly be monitored?

Third: Training language. Using a one-word command language, in a deep voice for authority and a high voice for praise and reward, is limited in scope and is not an entrance to your world of voice and sound communication. Your dog or cat will never learn you because you are not being yourself.

Fourth: Training theories and philosophies. When the above various and sundry training things don't seem to work, then everything is explained away and justified with profound-sounding excuses and denials.

You can become so bogged down in terminology, complex psychology, psychic theories, misinformation, comparisons to animals in the wild, gibberish, and useless gimmicks that then you are really up a creek without a paddle and no way out. *Ahhhhhh!* You are somewhere, but not where you want to be and you will never get to the heart of the matter.

This mind-bending and mind-altering type of training confuses the best of us. Just think how it sits with your dog or cat.

Fifth: Training experts. For dogs, we now see many new categories of trainers. There are trainers for puppies, trainers for passive dogs, trainers for aggressive dogs, trainers for depressed dogs, trainers for older dogs, and even trainers for trainers! These trainers teach paragraphs one to four.

When all training fails, it's over. Nobody wants these dogs or cats. And you know what eventually happens to them. What really gets our hair up is that these animals have never committed a crime, *but boy, have they been trained . . . to death.*

People who come to us with animal problems have all experienced "training" to some degree. But the whole spectrum of unacceptable behavior is still there: biting, barking, housebreaking, and destruction. Destructive dogs can be expensive to you, but aggressive dogs, dogs who attack and bite, can be out-and-out dangerous to everyone.

Then there are the dogs who have become frightened of life in general, of lightning, thunder, noises, cars, other dogs, and people. Never being able to relax and always being tense can make any healthy animal sick, including the human one. Frightened dogs must learn to trust you with their safety and security: this is the only way for them to calm down, relax, and not get sick or hurt. Frightened or nervous dogs can be a danger to themselves. A dog can panic while on a walk, bolt out into traffic, and it's good-bye, dog.

Let's not forget cats. What do you do when your cat is aggressive toward people or animals? Or your cat is frightened of anything and everything?

How do you keep your dog or cat from straying or wandering off? Besides locking or chaining them up.

These are all problems that we will be dealing with and solving quickly and without "training." You will see changes happening before your eyes, some immediately, and some in a few days. Our work involves understanding and redirecting behavior in a way that makes it simple for you to comprehend.

Wouldn't it be wonderful to read a book and then be able to apply the information in an easy, fun, practical way and have results quickly, successfully, and permanently? Without having to do all that work and practice required by "training"? That's the difference between teaching and training. The way Lee the cat taught Pickett the dog to stay away from his French toast.

You want answers? You want answers that work? And you want them fast? You'll get them. You will learn how to fit your dog or your cat into your life, do it in your own style, and in a way that's natural for you because you will get to the heart of the matter and not have to live a life of compromise.

To get to the heart of the matter you have to strip away all the layers of different "training" techniques and misinformation that were piled on top of your head, the original problems long forgotten in the morass of the more complex ones you are now stuck with. We will show you how to peel this onion without any tears. And it will all be done without any "training."

CHAPTER 4

Harmonic Triangle

Superior diet, pinpoint behavioral imprinting, right-on-target, crystal-clear information—these elements converge to form our harmonic, equilateral triangle. It's true that any one of these elements standing alone will give you answers to many problems, but to get the full benefits from our system, for all the parts to work in perfect harmony and to be permanent, the triangle must be balanced and complete. This harmonic-triangle philosophy will not only solve problems but will also prevent problems and put your dog and cat on track to a long, healthy, happy life.

These three elements, when absorbed and applied in total, will accentuate all the positive things you want from your dog or cat and eliminate all the negative ones. The harmonic triangle will put you, your dog, and your cat on a level of awareness that will give sensitivity a new meaning.

You will now get some real quality mileage out of that old

jalopy named Understanding. The triangle will put some high-octane gas, some oomph, into that tired and worn-out old roadster that has been running on empty for some time now and make Understanding mean something relevant in your life.

Even when you're looking through the rearview mirror of that old jalopy, you'll make a connection with your Soul Mirror, your cat and dog, especially if they're sitting comfortably in the backseat, being the superior, backseat drivers that they are.

When looking through a camera you have to focus the lens to see a clear picture. The same goes for someone needing glasses. To clear up your vision you get them. You marvel at what the world really looks like and how well you now can see it when you put on your new glasses. The picture we're clearing up and making easier for you to see is the one of you, your dog, and your cat.

This focused shaping will give you a whole new way of seeing these relationships working in concert.

Now that you are focused and have the all-seeing eyes of an eagle or a hawk, fly to the top of the pyramid and use this good vision to see with a whole new perspective, one that reaches far and wide. If hawks and eagles don't move you and all-seeing eyes aren't grabbing you either, then keep your eyes on your dollars; the harmonic triangle is rooted in economic good sense. We are going to save you lots of time, lots of effort, and lots of money, a bundle of it, and that ain't hay and it ain't birdseed either.

If you like the image of yourself standing on your pyramid, being master of all you survey, eagle-eyeing the world, here are a few things to ponder that might bring you down a peg or two, you eagle eye, you. Your dog and cat can see things with a clarity of vision you will never, ever see. They can hear sounds you will never, ever hear. They can even hear the sounds in the silence. They can feel, hear, and smell Mother Nature at work or at play even before she starts. They can read her mind. You can't. They know what's coming down the pike—earthquakes, hurricanes, storms, and tornadoes. You don't. You will never, ever be able to run as fast, jump as high, or be as graceful as your dog or cat. They are Olympic-class gold-medal athletes without any effort, practice, agents, or sponsors. The awesome power of your animals is their birthright, that's a given. So, you, you two-legged masters of the universe, put that information in your pipe and smoke it while driving your jalopy named Understanding.

Don't worry, take comfort in the fact that we're going to help you get on an almost equal footing with those other species, the super ones, those that are coexisting in your environment, so that at least those other superspecies will respect you enough to listen to you. In case you're not aware, those other species we're talking about are the cat and the dog. In case you're not aware, the environment we're talking about, that's where and how you live, your home and your lifestyle.

Now we will give you a key, one that only primates have access to. In case you weren't aware of what a primate is, you are a primate. Supposedly the dominant primate of these species. Maybe. We are going to give you an awesome power of your own—the harmonic triangle. One element of which we call the Magic Touch. This Magic Touch, wielded in the right hands and at the right time, gives everyday, ordinary objects an extraordinary life of their own. A pair of socks, laundered or not, the sneaker, designer or not, a magazine, current or old, will now become the aerodynamic tools of your future. You'll never again be able to look at these objects in quite the same way.

CHAPTER 5

Element One:
The Magic Touch

Your Own Supersense

Squirter and Spencer

Squirter and Spencer discover the relevance in their lives of the Austrian quantum theorist Erwin Schrödinger's hypothetical cat experiment. Or, how does an object exist in two places at the same time? These two experience firsthand a paradox of quantum physics at work.

"Spencer, you're not going to believe this. I was lying on the couch in the living room, just minding my own business, scratching one of my ears, the left one, the one that always seems to give me trouble, when Walter, all of a sudden, out of nowhere, calls me over to him. But I didn't feel like going, I wasn't in any mood to go, so I just continue scratching my ear. Then, bingo, out of nowhere, something hits me. I stop scratching. I jump up. It didn't hurt, but I mean, what a surprise! I mean it's strange for something to just fall on you like that, from right out of the blue. So, I took a whiff of what hit me. It whiffed like Walter! Spencer, it *was* Walter. Okay, okay, it was his glove, but it was Walter just the same, do you know what I mean? How was he able to reach me from all the way across the room, without even moving?"

Spencer the cat meowed, she couldn't believe her ears. "You mean to tell me that our Walter, from across the room, without moving, while sitting in his chair in a corner, at least twenty feet away from you, was able to reach over to the couch and glove you? Oh, no, no way, I don't believe that, this can't be. You're pulling my leg. His arms aren't that long. That's a lot of baloney."

Squirter, shushing Spencer, went on, "Wait, wait a minute, Spence, there's even more to this than meets the eye. You know how he always talks to us in that stupid one-word language? You know the one I'm talking about, that 'no, sit, stay, heel, come' language? Well, not anymore. He was talking to me like I'm one of his two-legged friends. Can you believe it?"

Spencer, stunned, but not wanting to show any look of astonishment, decided to turn away for a moment and explore her paws. "Come on, Squirter, you know Walter doesn't ever talk to us like he talks to his two-legged friends, we're just a cat and a dog to him. Nothing ever changes."

"Well, it has changed. But, hey, stop interrupting me, you always do that. You always cut me off. Now, let me finish!" Squirter snapped at Spencer. Then he continued, "He told me to come over to him. And I gave him the finger. And I ran upstairs and I went under the bed. And I figured at least there he'll leave me alone. He always does. No sooner do I close my eyes when here comes Walter! He reaches under the bed, grabs me by my collar, and without even a howdy-do and with not even a treat or nothing, he drags me allllll the way down those stairs, allllll the way across the living room, to where he first called me, and then he picks me up, hugs me and kisses me, and tells me what a good boy I am! And then he lets me go. I try to go back upstairs, but it turns out he's shut the door. So I just sit there by the door, thinking things over.

"Now here we are, just the two of us—me, a startled, tiny, little butterfly dog, thinking hard on what to do next, and Walter, a completely different side showing, a stranger. It looks like Walter, it smells like Walter, it sounds like Walter, but I tell you, Spencer, I'm thinking it's not Walter. It doesn't move like Walter anymore.

"We can get around, manipulate, and control our Walter because he can't do anything as good as we can. He's only got those silly people senses that don't work too good, and I ask you, how fast can he go standing up on those two legs? But this, I can't figure this out. I can't figure a way around this new throwing thing he's picked up. And you know I am a good figurer. Then it hits me, not the glove, the idea. It's Walter's doppelgänger, that's what it is. That's what I'm thinking we have here now."

Spencer's eyes grew to the size of saucers. All the hair on her body stood on end now, making her look at least twice her normal cat size. She thought to herself, *It's amazing, Squirter knowing about doppelgängers? Squirter knowing about Schrödinger's hypothetical cats?* She figured everyone had his double walking around somewhere on this planet, at least this seemed a theoretical possibility, on the level of quantum physics. Schrödinger proved this to be a reality and he had somehow taught his cat how to do this—to be in two places at the same time. But how could Squirter know about these scientific phenomena? And how did Walter learn quantum mechanics?

Maybe they're both smarter than I thought? Naaa, they must have seen it on some sci-fi TV show.

Squirter went on, "Then Walter's doppelgänger calls me again! He says to me in a soft, calm voice, 'Squirter, come over here.' I start to think about what I should do. Bingo, a glove hits me again. I think I better go to him, like the man asked me to. I get up and walk over to him. He must have given me ten seconds and I guess I musta took too long."

Spencer, unable to contain her excitement, took a swipe at Squirter and popped him one, right on the nose. "I don't believe this, what's gotten into Walter? Do me a favor, Squirter, hold that thought. I gotta take a leak. This is so exciting!"

Squirter, not wanting to hold it, walked along with Spencer over to her litter box. On the way he stopped for a quick squirt on Walter's slipper. *That'll learn him*, Squirter thought to himself. Then, feeling better, he continued his tale, "Once more he called me over. Let me tell you, Spencer, I didn't know what to do. Where to turn. Where to run. But, I remembered when I went to him he was nice to me. So, carefully, one step at a time, like negotiating a minefield, I slowly and silently made my way over to Walter. And what do you think he did?"

Spencer was beside herself. "What, Squirter, what? What could this mad man, this doppelgänger do? Were you in any danger at any time?"

Squirter enjoyed exciting the cat. He loved Spencer's large eyes on him in rapt attention. "Well, let me tell you what he did, let me tell you exactly what he did. He picked me up, gave me a big, fat kiss, and told me what a good boy I was! And then he carried me into the kitchen and gave me a nice chunk of tasty, herb-roasted turkey."

Spencer was all ears, nose, and eyes now. "What the hell is that? What in the hell is tasty, herb-roasted turkey, Squirter?

My stuff is always the same stuff, the dry stuff with the artificial guck that dries like concrete. Yuck. I hate it, but that's all he ever gives me. I gotta tell ya, that tasty, herb-roasted turkey sounds real cool to me. The next time he gives you that stuff, make sure you bring me some!"

Squirter, being the nice little butterfly dog that he was, generously agreed. "And, anyway, let me go on, Spencer. Now I'm eating my tasty, herb-roasted turkey chunks, enjoying my good fortune, when out of nowhere, from the other room, Walter calls me again. That sly son of a gun, the minute I get into my turkey he sneaks out. 'Hey, Squirter, get in here!' First, I thought about running upstairs, but I figured he'll come and get me. Then I thought about hiding elsewhere, but he's got this new attitude. You-can-run-but-you-can't-hide attitude. And he's got this new magic and that new longer than life reach of his, like the fantastic stretching abilities of Plastic Man, the super comic-book hero in Walter's old comic books. It's useless. Anyway, I was thinking it through, what to do, when I quickly realized from my past experience of the last fifteen minutes that I only had about ten seconds to make up my mind. So I went to him. He picked me up again, kissed me again, and took me back in the kitchen again and gave me another chunk of tasty, herb-roasted again, for being, as he said, 'such a gooood little boy!' Now, I gotta tell you, Spencer, every time this guy calls me I'm going to listen. Why not? It doesn't hurt, he's not going to bite me when I come to him. I guess he's just trying to tell me, when he wants me, I go. I can understand that, and I think it's only fair." Squirter gave Spencer a digestive moment. A moment to reflect on this new regime, before dropping another bombshell.

"Guess what Walter told me when we had our dinner together last night?" Squirter said nonchalantly.

Spencer butted in again. "You had dinner together?"

"Yes, we had the same thing, I ate what Walter ate—jumbo shrimp marinara, spaghetti, and broccoli rabe, sautéed in olive oil and garlic."

Spencer could not contain herself. "Jumbo shrimp! That's an oxymoron!"

Squirter, jumping up and down now, was getting uncontrollably annoyed. "You butted in again! And I'll tell you something, oxymoron, shmoxymoron, I don't care how smart or stupid they were, they tasted fantastic! Now, be quiet, Spencer, be quiet and let me talk."

Finally calming down a bit, Squirter continued, "And then we talked things over, over dinner, Walter and I did. It was nice, a pleasant tête-à-tête. Walter said to me, 'Listen, Squirter, from now on things are going to be different around here, they're going to change for the better. This is my new contract with you. Here's how it's going to be. When I call you, you come to me. You will have ten seconds to make up your mind as to what you are going to do. I will always give you time to think things through. I will no longer talk to you in a silly one-word language. You will learn my language. If you don't come to me after ten seconds, I will toss something at you. It's called my Magic Touch. You see, Squirter, I know that even for a little guy, you know a lot more than people think you do. And so does your buddy Spencer. I know that you and Spencer have always felt that with your supersenses, you didn't have to listen to anything I said or do anything I wanted because I wasn't as good as you two. That's been up until now.

"'I know I'm limited in certain areas, that my nose, my ears, and my eyes don't work as well as yours do, and they probably never will. And that you, as the masters of body language, also know the limits of my reach and what I can physically accomplish. Well, that's all changed now, that's all in the past. You have now been introduced to the secret of us primates. I have a Magic Touch, the ability to reach you from anywhere, at any distance and at any time.'

"What do you think of that, Spencer? I'll tell you something, I never knew Walter had such potential, such inner strength and such wisdom. Walter is smarter than we thought he was. He makes me feel so secure and so special now."

"I'm shocked, absolutely. That sure doesn't sound like our Walter. Wow!" blew Spencer. Stroking the air with her tail, Spencer mused, "What about me? This golden Abyssinian child you see. Do you think he'll leave this great cat be?"

Squirter, impressed as always by Spencer's poetic musings, scratched his behind and considered. "Well, I don't know, Spence. As you say, you are a great, gifted, golden cat. Nothing is supposed to work with you exalted ones. Everyone knows that. But who knows? We're talking a new Walter here. There could be more surprises on the horizon. Maybe even for a night walker, an Abyssinian we all know so well."

In the games of life, who would be the winner? Would Spencer be free to pursue her time-honored nocturnal rambles? Or would she have to sleep, perchance to dream, each night from then on? Spencer, this cat who walked by night, this cool cat walking, would she have to mend her ways and respect the rights of others, give them a break, a good night's sleep after all? Who would be the winner in this game of night moves?

As if a time-out had been called, the cat and the dog stared at each other—contemplating the rhetorical questions that hung heavily in the air and the uncertain future that lay waiting for them and especially for Spencer, the Abyssinian Night Walker.

... Later That Same Evening

Sleep wouldn't come for Spencer. But sleep had taken Walter and Squirter some hours ago. Next to her, Walter and Squirter, sharing the same pillow, were nose to nose, snoring away in a melodious, singsong a cappella, Squirter carrying the high notes and Walter the low.

Lying on her back, Spencer stared at the ceiling, watching the shadows of the night play there. When she was sure Walter and Squirter were deep into dreamland, she followed her uncontrollable urges to know the night and all its forbidden secrets, to know what was hidden within the darkness. She rolled over, got up, jumped off the bed, and decided to take a walkabout. When she wanted to think things through, night rambles always did it for her. She walked for hours, but the answers continued to elude her. Not a clue could she glean from anywhere, she couldn't figure out the secret of the primates. The ability to throw. Why? It was frustrating, so very frustrating. She decided the best thing to do was to go back to bed. Maybe tomorrow night the answers would come.

Upon jumping effortlessly onto the bed, she figured a little paw kneading and some creative stretching would do her some good. She enjoyed these isometric exercises thoroughly and meowed with great pleasure.

All of a sudden, out of nowhere, something hit her. She jumped straight up in the air. When she came down, she smelled Walter. The smell was unmistakable. It *was* Walter. Well, it wasn't Walter exactly, it was his slipper, his soft corduroy one. Squirter, who had been woken up by the noise, looked over to Spencer and said, "Now you know what I'm talking about." Spencer asked Squirter where was her chunk of tasty herb-roasted? Wasn't the herb-roasted supposed to come to her after she was magically touched? Squirter couldn't answer, he had already fallen back into a deep sleep. A slight smile was on his face.

Spencer circled the slipper, walked away from the slipper, came back to the slipper, sat on the slipper, pushed the slipper around a little bit with her paws, and finally just fell on it and went to sleep. The last thing she heard before dozing off was her Walter saying, "Good girl."

What had once been hearsay was now fact. Spencer got her tasty herb-roasted in the morning. From then on, all three of them ate great-tasting, good, fresh food. When the urge to night walk was irresistible, Spencer walked, but she did so silently, without disturbing her friends. The Magic Touch saw to it that she let sleeping friends lie, sleeping.

Attitude

Your attitude toward your dog is as important as how you use the Magic Touch. Teaching your dog to come to you is the most important lesson he will ever learn. His life might depend on it one day. This lesson is crucial because it gives you the confidence of knowing that you have complete control of your dog under any and all circumstances and in any emergency. You want him. You call him. He comes to you. He's safe. Period, end of discussion. Therefore, your attitude has to reflect the seriousness of your actions.

Teaching your dog to come to you is not a game; the Magic Touch is not a game either. It is the necessary lifesaving tool that will teach your dog to come to you and to listen to you.

On a national network television show we asked Tina to toss a magazine at her six-month-old golden retriever, Schatzi, and then to call her. Tina did, but at first her way of throwing was playful and not serious. Possibly, being in front of the television cameras intimidated Tina. Cameras have the ability to make people feel a bit nervous and insecure. Insecurity and indecision will show up big time as a sign of weakness in your dog's eyes and nose because your dog is the true expert on body language, and what the eyes don't see, the nose knows.

Schatzi felt that she didn't have to listen to her nervous Tina and so she didn't. But when Tina finally got tired of being embarrassed by Schatzi, who was screwing up their television debut, and at last threw her magazine with true meaning, true love, true aim, and some gusto, Schatzi immediately came over to her.

The whole sequence, including the time it took for Tina's total transformation from fooling around to serious business, took no more than fifteen minutes. If you take what you're doing seriously, others will, too, and in short order.

The Tools of the Trade

It's easiest to start off in a small room. You sit down and relax. Make sure you have something to throw. If you have a young puppy, a clean slate as we like to call these brand-new additions to the world, a pair of rolled-up socks will do just fine. If you have an older puppy with bad habits or with a mind of his own, or an adult dog with even more of both, then you will need something more substantial in the way of a mind changer. A sneaker is fine, it's soft and won't hurt. A magazine is also fine. You'll have to decide size, but use more not less. We're not looking to hurt the dog, but we also don't want him to think we're playing around or that it is game time.

We got a call from a woman in Virginia. She wanted to know why her Great Dane hadn't come to her and wouldn't listen to her when she threw something at him. We asked her what she had chosen as a tossing tool. We were surprised at her answer. Her tool of choice was a Ping-Pong-ball-sized, spongy Nerf-ball toy that belonged to her cat. Too small. Small wonder it didn't work.

On the phone we asked her if she was wearing sneakers. When she said she was, we asked her to take one sneaker off and toss it at her great big Great Dane, using a little muscle. She did. He came to her.

Remember, by your increasing the velocity of your throw your dog will know that this is not a game you're playing. If he starts to play with what you threw, you are not throwing substantially enough.

Once your dog learns this technique and listens to you, then if you want to, you can use the Virginia Nerf-ball technique and your dog will still listen to you, even if he is the greatest of Great Danes or the smallest of magnificent, mighty mini-dogs.

The Language

Call your dog once, don't repeat yourself. Use a sentence. "Squirter, come over here." Give him ten seconds to respond. It takes that long for the message to be sent, to be received, and then to be acted on. If he doesn't come to you, throw your chosen object. It must touch him. When it hits him, he will smell it. On it will be your unique smell, the one he already knows, your salt and nitric acid. Your dog, like any freethinker worth his salt, will decide on one of three options that are available to him.

Option number one. He will come to you. If that's the case, grab him by the collar and tell him how good he is. Give him a hug and a kiss. Or, if that's not your style, shake his hand. Make sure that you have hold of your dog before you tell him how good he is. If you praise him before he gets to you, then he might think halfway is close enough and good enough.

Option number two. He might decide not to move at all. Go to him quietly, don't say a word, take him by the collar, pull him allllll the way to where you were when you first called him over. When you get back to where you first called him from, then tell him how good he is. Even if he wasn't. The object is to let him know what you want of him.

Option number three. This is the most popular option for the four-legged beginners who learn the way of the Magic Touch. They run away. That's what they do. Now you can see why we use a small room with a closed door for the first-time toss. If your dog runs away, quietly go get him, take him by his collar, and pull him alllll the way back to where you were when you first called him. Then tell him what a good boy he was for coming to you on his own, even if he didn't and you had to pull him all the way over.

His options will always be those three, but there will be variations on these themes. For example, your dog might only come halfway to you when you call him. Halfway is no way at all. Get him by the collar and pull him alllll the way to you. Another variation could be that he of the superior hearing might pretend he didn't hear you. Don't buy into these themes. Continue working until he comes to you. This should never take you more than half an hour. And your dog or puppy does have a good memory, but sometimes it becomes a selective one.

Commitment

If for any reason you have to stop—the phone rings, the apple pie in the oven is burning, you're getting tired, or you feel your dog is getting tired—you still have to complete what you started. So complete it quickly. Call your dog. If he doesn't come to you, go get him, pull him over to you, and tell him he's great, then go take care of the pie or answer the phone or take a nap. Never let your dog think that distractions mean he's off the hook in any way, shape, or form. Finish what you start, it's imperative.

All conversations with your dog should end on a positive note; that is, with your dog listening to you in one way or another. That means with him always coming to you or being pulled to you or listening to whatever it is that you have to say to him.

Still, teaching your dog to come to you our way never, ever takes longer than an hour in total. And it usually takes half that time. If it's taking you longer than an hour to complete this lesson, something might not be clear in your communication line. So stop, take a step back, and think through what the obstacle could be.

Don't increase the work area until your dog comes to you in the small, designated space. Once he learns to come to you, then you can increase the distance and open up the whole house. He must come to you from upstairs, downstairs, from anywhere. If he doesn't, and he uses all of his themes in variation to wear you down, so you might give up on getting him to listen to you, especially the theme that you won't come all the way upstairs and get him out from under the bed, show your dog he's all wrong about you. When you make a commitment, you will follow through on it even if it takes you to the ends of the earth and time. So, going upstairs won't seem like such a big deal. It is only upstairs, after all. Your dog must learn that he can run but he can't hide, and once he learns that, he won't run or hide because to do either would be pointless.

Don't test your dog outside until he is coming to you 100 percent of the time in the house—until he is coming to you even if there are other distractions or interferences, both well meant or annoying, such as people, cats, dogs, food, or anything else around that might get him away from you, including turtles. We love turtles. They wear pretty earth tones, they don't bite, and they don't go fast. Your dog must come to you no matter what other attention-getting forces are around to distract either of you.

If your dog won't listen to you inside, where you do have some degree of control, he is certainly not going to listen to you at all when you are outside. Outside, the minute he gets a noseful of fresh air and the taste of freedom, and where there are no boundaries to keep him in line, he's gone, he's off to the races. You will lose all control of him. So make sure you've got it all together, that he is listening to you 100 percent, inside, before you teach him to come to you, outside.

When outside, it's a good idea to first start in an enclosed area, such as a tennis court or a fenced-in backyard, just to make sure that when you take a walk out into the wild blue yonder, your dog will still be with you and that he will come back to you when you call him or if you throw something. If he does listen, then you're in business. If he doesn't, then you make him come back to you and you are still in business.

Teach him step by step by step. It's easy and it's fun. It's easy because it works so fast. It's fun because you can actually see your dog thinking things through and working them out.

All parents enjoy watching their children achieve. All teachers enjoy their students' successes and accomplishments.

Your dog is much smarter than you think, and he's now exercising a most important part of his body, his brain, thereby forging his way to a higher consciousness.

Be careful not to let your dog know anything about your business, your investments, or your banking, because with all this new brainpower he's acquiring, he might just look to step into your shoes, instead of eating them.

Remember, teaching this principle should be quick, a half hour or so; it's not days, weeks, months, years, to teach your dog to come to you. But this is the number one behavior that you must teach your pal.

Once your dog knows how to do this, don't practice it. Do it for real. If he's running and you want him back and you call him and he doesn't listen to you, you throw, it works. This powerful and versatile tool, the Magic Touch, will prove invaluable to you.

A Walk, a Run, a Toss, It's Done

Contrary to what you might think, teaching your dog to walk or to run along with you without a leash is simple. It's only an extension of what he's already learned. You want to teach him to focus on you and the walk or run at hand. When you've taught your dog the ways of the Magic Touch and he's listening to you all the time, it's literally a hop, skip, and jump to have him run along with you.

Here it is. First, you take a walk with your dog. You have to learn to walk before you can run. If he goes out ahead of you, you throw and stop. Give him time to think through what you want of him. If he doesn't come back to you, then call him back to you. When he comes over to you, touch him first and then tell him how good he is.

Start walking again. If your dog goes out too far, throw and stop again. This time, don't call him. Let the Magic Touch tell him that he shouldn't have strayed in the first place. At this point, he should come back on his own, without being told anything. This next step is to teach him not to leave you until you tell him he can. By throwing and not telling him anything if he runs out, he will learn to stay with you. This silent means of communication, the Magic Touch, is extremely persuasive.

If your dog comes over to you, praise him. If he doesn't, go and get him by his collar and pull him back to you. Praise him for that. The object here is to teach your dog to walk or to jog at your side, and to only go out when you tell him that it's okay to do so.

Your next move. To show your dog that you are multidirectional, that you are capable of going backward as well as forward, you now take a step backward. If he follows you, praise him. If he doesn't and you can reach him, give him a slight pop on the behind with the back of your hand, just to let him know that he should be paying attention to you. If you can't reach him with your hand when you step back, throw, toss the Touch.

Give him some time to think through what you want; he should step backward along with you. If he is not where you want him, then make sure you place him where you do want him, before you tell him how good he is.

The main objective of this exercise is to make sure that your dog keeps you in his peripheral vision. Do this until he gets the idea. He will. Now you can walk forward, backward, make turns, and even stop on a dime and he will be with you like your shadow.

Another exercise we like is to take a step and stop. And take a step and stop, forward or backward. Your dog should be following every step of the way. This is like teaching him how to dance by the numbers, sort of like a step-by-step tango.

He'll enjoy this because you are giving him your undivided attention, and he'll be watching your every move with great interest. You're making him think about you and your next moves. This is a good game as far as we are concerned, because it is an educational one, it teaches him the many ways that a person can walk and run. You've now taught your dog how to walk without a leash.

Running is the same principle. Go running and be prepared to throw if your dog does not have you in his peripheral vision. That means he's too far away from you. When you throw, you can either stop or you can keep running. He must learn that he has to stay with you.

If he decides to lag behind, turn around and throw. Don't let him get away from you with any of his own creative running, because you could both run into problems.

Once your dog learns to keep you in his peripheral vision, you can run with him, you can walk with him, you can go hiking with him, swimming, anything you want when you are on the move. You'll now have good company instead of an uncontrollable dog. Remember, everything must start at home.

Don't take your dog out to run in extreme temperatures. His fur coat is a killer in the summer. He'd prefer air-conditioning. In the winter rain and cold, he would prefer to be where it is warm and dry.

Don't make him run along with you or pull you when you are on a bike or Rollerblades; he'll do it for you because he is a loyal friend, but he won't enjoy it, it isn't his cup of tea to be forced to participate in your folly. He might get hurt.

When you're out with your dog, he's your responsibility— more important than how many miles you've logged and how quickly you've logged them.

You can do a few things for your dog if you are taking him out for a run. Push him along in one of those three-wheel baby-jogging carriers in case he decides to take a nap. He'll love riding along with the wind in his ears and you using your people power to motor him.

You know your run isn't the most exciting thing in his life. Bring a bottle of spring water in case he gets thirsty, a nice tuna-fish sandwich in case he gets hungry. You might decide to run ten or fifteen miles, or all day, so make sure you have an umbrella attachment to keep the sun off him. Bring along a good book for him to read, or if he is not a reader of books, maybe some comics will suffice.

But whatever you choose for him, keep in mind he does not relish the thought of running an iron man's triathlon every day, even if that's your bag.

Warning Signs

Don't warn your dog that you are going to throw something, just throw it. This mental lag on your part, this hesitation to throw and commit yourself, will cost you. If you start by warning your dog that you are going to throw, he's going to take off on you. That warning will be all the clue he needs to leave before you can act. Remember, he's faster than you and he doesn't have a hesitation or commitment problem.

He who hesitates is lost, and the winner is long gone. By the time you've thought it over to throw, what to throw, by the time you've poised yourself to throw, he's already committed himself to leave and he will.

Warning him will become the trigger point for him to take off before you get the chance to throw. You might not realize this but he does. This master of body language will learn another clue to besting you.

The definition of a split second will be from the time it takes you to raise your arm to throw to the time your dog takes off. It's the surprise effect and the contact of the throw that counts. With the Magic Touch you're holding four aces, so don't give your hand away so easily by warning him. Surprise him.

The Magic Touch is the key. Your dog must know that you can and will reach him from anywhere and at any time, and without warning. You have to be the one he always looks to and depends on, his guiding light. By throwing, you reveal your awesome powers. Once taught this, your dog will become a true believer and never want to go elsewhere.

Two cardinal rules: Never call your dog and punish him, and

never let anyone else, ever, use this Magic Touch on your dog. It's only to be used by you and whoever is in your immediate family unit.

The Touch Control for Bad Habits

Once your dog knows to come to you with the Magic Touch throw, it's only a short step, a variation on our principle theme of the Magic Touch, to convince your dog to mend his wicked ways. Barking, biting, fighting, jumping, or any catch-him-in-the-act bad habits are stopped immediately, if not sooner.

He jumps, you throw; when he stops, you tell him how wonderful he is. He barks, you throw; when he stops, you tell him how marvelous he is.

Never say "no" or "sit " when stopping a wicked way. They don't work. What they will do is work against the throwing technique. The throwing will stop your dog; the "no" won't do a damn thing, as you all know from experience. And the "no" and the throwing together will confuse the best of us, because that becomes a confusing double negative.

Your dog is barking, you're getting a headache. You throw your magazine or your sneaker, depending on the size of your dog. Remember, we're not looking to hurt him, but we also are not looking to make this a game. We're just looking to stop his noise and our headache. Don't say anything, just throw and surprise the hell out of him. He will stop barking, smell the magazine or sneaker, and you then tell him he's great for listening to you and stopping his barking. If he doesn't stop, do it again, and again and again, until he stops. He will. This is more commitment on your part, not to stop, until he does.

Don't corner your dog, it isn't constructive. It will work against what you are trying to do. Always give him a way out, somewhere to go. For example, if he is in a corner or in a closet, step back a few feet, go to one side of where he is, and throw from there. Don't stand on top of him when you are throwing. You want your dog to make the right decision. And if you are in his face, you're giving him no choice. The only decision he can make will not be to your liking.

When you're throwing to stop a bad habit, don't call your dog either. You're not interested in his coming to you now, you are interested in stopping something that he's doing that is unacceptable to you.

You want to make your dog stop doing whatever it is that you don't want, and that's it. If he does come to you, that's fine, too. Touch him, give him a kind word, or spoil him rotten, but he doesn't have to come to you in this case.

For example, you made him stop barking. He walks away to lie down somewhere, that's okay. If he wants to go away and sulk because you made him stop his annoying nonsense, that's okay, too. If he wants to call all of his friends and complain about you to them, that's perfectly okay with us.

Just remember, most dogs have relatives abroad: French poodles, English setters, Tibetan mastiffs, Italian greyhounds, Russian borzoi, and so forth and so on. If you allow your dog to use the phone, make sure he pays for his own calls because they could very well be long-distance and he could very well be on the phone for some time. Those who love to complain usually complain an awful lot.

Do not use the Magic Touch throwing technique to teach your dog to sit down, to lie down, or to go away from you. This is only to be used to teach your dog to come to you or to stop any annoying, destructive, or dangerous problems that you are seeing and experiencing firsthand.

Mona, Morris, and the Pot

Mona lives with a jumping Jack. He is not a kangaroo, not a rabbit, and not a frog either. In fact his name isn't even Jack. It's Morris, and he is a little white dog who loves to jump and has taken his sport of jumping to new heights. As Mona complained, "I can't even come in the door. I can't put my packages down. I can't put my purse down. I can't take my coat off. He jumps all over me. What should I do?"

Two years ago when we first met a frantic and nervous Mona in her small studio, it was hard to find this mini Maltese puppy. Oh, yes, he certainly was a mini, you had to weigh him on a dieter's food scale to get an accurate weight.

But that wasn't the reason he was hard to find. It was because this small studio apartment was subdivided by an enormous doggy crate sized for a Great Dane or Saint Bernard, several fifty-pound bags of dry puppy food, the highest-priced, largest doggy carry bag available, and three four-foot-high, state-of-the-art separator gates to further divide and restrict Morris's movements.

Mona, who appeared somewhat shell-shocked by her new and first-time responsibilities as a mother, and lost amid the doggy trimmings, was overwhelmed. Keep in mind Mona is only a foot taller than the gates. She moved like a somnambulist through this maze of doggy training apparatus, knocking into things and from time to time tripping and disappearing from view altogether.

One could only wonder about the salesperson who had convinced Mona that all of these "les must, essentials" were necessary. Had our Mona been an easy mark? After we helped her get back into the world of common sense, she was relieved to be able to return everything posthaste to the East Side designer pet shop from whence it all had come, getting back the $2,000 that she had shelled out for the restrictive gimmicks and controlling paraphernalia that had corralled and caged both Mona and Morris. She didn't have a problem with her return because none of this stuff had been on sale.

Perhaps the stuff should have been given to a state or federal correctional facility, because from what we've read they are overcrowded and underfunded and might have some use for it.

But Morris was a different story. This bighearted, two-pound puppy, weighing in at $500 a pound, was worth every penny. Mona had even felt extremely fortunate, for Morris had been on sale.

Now, two years later, Morris had decided to embark on this new jumping career. All Mona needed was to be reminded of how to use the Magic Touch to stop Morris from happily jumping all over her when she came home from work. More than a reminder, Mona needed to be fortified and supported because she was of two minds. Mind number one said, "I want to stop this, it's become a major headache, and it's causing runs in all of my stockings." Mind number two said, "I'm gone all day, he misses me, he loves me so much, how can I stop him from showing all of this affection? It might not be fair to him."

To set both of her minds at ease we assured her that Morris would still love her, he would just stop jumping. We made the exercise simple and direct. You come home from work. You take the elevator up to your floor. You find something to throw, something soft, your wallet or your eyeglass case. Get it into your hand. With your other hand open the door to your apartment . When he jumps, throw at him. He will smell the object thrown. He will stop the jumping. If he doesn't, pick up the object and throw it again. Do not say, "No." Don't say anything to him until he stops. When he stops, tell him he is a good boy for not jumping. That was what Mona was supposed to do.

Determined, Mona got herself all revved up for the Morris-missile mission. Going over the steps in her mind, over and over, she worked herself up. She didn't want to forget anything. She got into her elevator. She made a selection, her soft leather, Gucci eyeglass case. She felt comfortable with her choice: the case had balance and she felt sure of its accuracy.

The doors closed and up she went. Higher and higher and each floor bringing her closer and closer to her objective, and Mona more and more resolved to the confrontation. Mona didn't have the congress or Senate to debate this one-strike mission. She didn't have Stealth bombers, fighter jets, radar, or smart bombs. She had her Gucci case, her Magic Touch, her only hope for a quick victory. Morris was going to stop jumping this day. For sure.

The elevator stopped. Mona, fully charged, got off and went quietly down the hall. She grabbed the doorknob, the door was unlocked. She stepped in and threw simultaneously. The eyeglass case flew across the room and hit. It was a bull's-eye. She hit her target straight on. There were only a few problems. The first being that Mona had entered the wrong apartment. The second being, she had thrown at a flowerpot. The flowerpot, and the plant it held, never jumped on anybody again. We can guarantee you that it became the best-behaved flowerpot on East Seventy-sixth Street.

The couple who lived in the apartment, who happened to be home watching television, were surprised to see Mona in their living room and attacking their flowerpot. But, hey, this is New York. Whatever.

Downstairs, Morris continues to jump happily and is happily jumping to this day. Mona, all the wind gone from her sails, has made her peace with the situation. "Morris just loves to jump. So let him jump! As long as he loves me."

Learning is one thing and applying it is another. Rationalizing is a third thing. And one person, being of two minds, could be many things.

Cats and the Magic Touch

The Magic Touch works extremely well for all kinds of problems you might be experiencing with your cat. Putting an end to aggression, nighttime annoyances, and all sorts of "I see what you're doing" types of bad behavior can easily be solved by applying the Magic Touch. Use the touch in exactly the same way as you would with your dog.

If you want to teach your cat to come to you, it's the same way as teaching your dog. Only you'll have to exercise a little more patience and time, because cats imprint behaviorally much earlier than dogs do and have well-established habit patterns, from an early age, ones that they don't like to give up too easily. Felines, after all, are the ultimate "cat's meow" and don't like to change their elusive, mysterious, independent ways.

Since your cat is a creature of the night and might bother you when you're sleeping, tell him not to do it. Here's how. The sequence is, your cat wakes you up, you throw something, the something touches him, he stops what he's doing, he smells it. You tell him he's good, if you want; if you don't want, just go back to sleep. That's it.

If you have an aggressive cat and he likes to attack other cats, dogs, people, big or small ones—throw. It's over, and it's over fast. Don't forget to tell your cat how good he is when he stops being nasty. You'll see significant changes in the elusive, mysterious one once he learns you, too, have a supersense.

Hollywood Cat

This Hollywood producer we know has a cat. She's a large black cat with puffy white feet. The producer complained that the cat was dysfunctional and a real bitch. No matter how much love she poured out on the cat, the cat ignored her completely. The cat only appeared from various hiding places to eat, go to the toilet, or to annoy our Hollywood producer. At night this cat slept "butt side" in her producer's face. No respect whatsoever.

We had stopped by to take a meeting and take a lunch. That's show-biz talk, if you must know. During this meeting we were taking, the cat showed up from time to time. She walked back and forth at a distance, eyeing us curiously, and then with an enigmatic wink and a grin she'd disappear.

While puffing away on her fourth or fifth cigarette in as many minutes, the smoky Hollywood producer said with knowing conviction, "She will never come in here to join us, she hates me. This cat has hated me from the day we met. It's been only three years, but it seems like an eternity. God! But why? Why does she hate me? She avoids me like the plague; this cold-shoulder treatment really pisses me off. What have I ever done to her to deserve this?

"I buy her everything. I buy her the best cat food money can buy, I buy her the A-list doctors. And what about the emerald collar I bought her from Winston's? The one she wore for my Academy Awards party. That set me back a pretty penny. She was gorgeous and she blended in perfectly with my green champagne flutes."

Hollywood paused and considered for a moment the unfairness of life and how ungrateful her cat was after all she had done for her and bought for her.

"This cat has not one, but two litter boxes; in case she gets tired of one, she'll have the other one to use. I know that everyone needs two bathrooms, that's the way it is.

"Meanwhile, here she is a cat with everything, including two bathrooms of her own, so why, I ask you, why does she have to go into mine?" At this point, Hollywood was so distressed that she stopped for yet another cigarette, not remembering that she had one already dangling from her lips. While pacing nervously, she poured herself a drink, spilling half of it and not paying any mind to the staining spill.

The cat crossed again in the background, and the producer turned and gave her a dirty look. "Witch!" she hissed. The cat didn't even blink. Hollywood could have been invisible for all this cat cared.

Hollywood went on with her tale of unrequited love and treachery. "So, the party was in full swing. And I admit, I admit, I was wrapped up in the success of this wonderful Awards party and wasn't aware of where the cat was. But that's not unusual, I never know where this cat is, I never see this damn cat. So why should I have even thought that this cat was conspiring to screw up my party and my life as well? But, she managed, she managed to do both. Boy, oh boy, did she blow it for me, and big time!

"My biggest moneyman, my meal ticket to the top, went in to use my bathroom. I guess he wanted to freshen up, to use the toilet, to wash his hands, whatever. What do men do in the bathroom? They do what they do. The next thing I hear is this bloodcurdling scream, banging, slamming, and cursing. Then, out flies Kenneth Gleason, holding his white silk dinner jacket in one hand. It was shredded and dripping yellow. In the other hand he carried his satin loafer and held up his torn pants. His face, his hands, and any other part of exposed anatomy were covered by tracks of bloody claw marks. His face had the horrified look of death.

"He turned for a minute, looked at me, pointed his finger at me, shaking it, and telling me, 'to go and f --- myself, I don't ever want to see you again, I don't ever want to talk to you again, you'll never work in this town again [show-biz threat], and that goes double for that vicious, no-good, mirror-image, ##$$***ing cat of yours, as well!'

"With that, Kenneth Gleason turned and stormed out the door. The seat of his pants, now revealed for all to see, was torn and bloodied. The shredded cloth, flapping like a battle-scarred flag in the wind, waved a sad and final good-bye to all.

"At first, about a hundred partying people stood frozen in silence. The only thing you could hear was the television playing in the background, telling us someone won the award for the best editor of a foreign short subject. Who cares about short subjects? My life just went down the toilet!

"Now, out of that very same bathroom comes that cat, that bitch! Up onto the smorgasbord she jumps and starts to enjoy the smoked salmon, the chicken livers, the shrimp cocktail, and the beluga caviar as if nothing had happened. Her tail moved back and forth and back and forth as she happily ate all that expensive food.

"The frozen people seemed locked on that moving tail, as if they were an orchestra ready and waiting for direction. Then the cat, fat and stuffed to the gills, belched and slowly left the table.

"All the frozen party people suddenly defrosted. It started with whispers, then lots of laughing and loud noise, then it all reached a boiling crescendo of pandemonium.

"I'm sure it was all directed towards me, this laughing and noise, people love to see a disaster in the making. And, of course, since Kenneth Gleason left, everyone wanted to leave. No one wants to get on his bad side. I was now like a pariah! They couldn't wait to abandon my sinking ship.

"I screamed and told everybody to get out, out of my house, now! Friggin' freeloaders, eating my caviar, drinking my champagne! Who needs 'em! Well, they all left me. My nearest and dearest, my hundred closest friends. Now, I would have nothing and nobody but that cat, who hates me.

"I was in tears. I didn't know what to do or what to think. All

I did was collapse and cry myself to sleep. The last thing I remembered, before passing out, was that *Titanic* got another award. I won an award too, an award for the worst night I've ever had in my whole life.

"When I woke up in the morning, there she was, with her butt in my face as usual and as if last night had never, ever happened.

"I found out a few days later from a sycophantic servant, assistant, of Kenneth Gleason that what had happened was this: Kenneth Gleason had walked into the bathroom, locked the door, taken his jacket off, and laid it properly folded across a chair. When he turned to sit down, he must have stepped on the cat's tail; it seems she had been hanging out in the bathroom. Why? I couldn't tell you. Then all hell broke loose. The cat was all over him in a matter of seconds.

"Kenneth Gleason, surprised and terrified, jumped up screaming. He tripped over his pants in his panic and fell down, ripping them. One of his shoes came off when he fell. He was so overcome by fright, he was in such a state of panic, that picking himself up off the floor became a life-and-death struggle. With his adrenaline pump going at top speed, he grabbed his shoe and his pants and his jacket and with the cat still in hot pursuit and shredding him, he flew out of the bathroom and out of my house. That witch! That's the last straw. Out. I want her out of my life altogether!"

Reliving the painful experience, Hollywood collapsed on the couch and started bawling. "Look how she treats me, this ungrateful SOB. I come home, I open the door, I expect her to greet me, she's never there. When I'm having a tough day and I'm upset or angry, she doesn't care. All she wants to do is eat and eat and drink, and she lets me know that. After dinner, she throws up hair balls in my very best shoes and I never find out about the hair balls until I put them on."

We handed Hollywood her soft pack of cigarettes and told her to throw them at the cat the next time she saw her. She looked at us as if we were crazy. She said, "I can't do that, the cat will hate me, and anyway she's not here." At that very moment, Providence intervened: the cat made one of her rare appearances.

Reluctantly, Hollywood threw the soft pack, reasoning that the cat hated her anyway, so the situation couldn't get any worse. We thought we saw a little smile break across the producer's face as she let fly the soft pack. We felt some payback was being sent along with the soft pack.

The soft pack hit. The cat jumped, took off, came back in a matter of seconds, smelled the cigarette pack, walked around it, sat down next to it, and within five minutes decided to come over and sit with us. The producer was dumbfounded. She fell back on her couch in total shock and disbelief. For the first time ever, our producer called her cat by name, which happened to be Greta G.

A few days later Hollywood called us from her car, while taking a drive with Greta G. She was ecstatic about the way this "touch healing therapy," as she described it, had been fabulously successful. She felt she had experienced a major breakthrough and gotten in touch with Greta G.'s higher self, or at least that is what her analyst's analysis was. She told us that Greta G. since being touch-healed was sharing the bed, cuddling and purring away, as if she'd been Hollywood's pal for years.

Now Greta G. is always waiting at the door when Hollywood comes home, and they spend much significant, quality time together. So much for "I vant to be alone." Oh, yes, the hair balls are not in the shoes anymore. Fresh food also works wonders and saves many pairs of shoes.

Hollywood went on in glowing terms about her new insights

and revelations, her discoveries about the cat's phenomenal, life-affirming transformation. She also felt that the cat had made her a better person. A person with sensitivities to others.

Then, she said something surprisingly out of character, sensitive and quite thoughtful: "I guess you can't buy love or loyalty from a cat."

"You can't buy it from a dog either," we liked to add. "Love and loyalty should be earned, not paid for."

"I don't have a dog," Hollywood said pointedly. "I have a cat, as anyone with eyes can plainly see. Why are you talking about dogs?" And then, stepping back into character, the Hollywood we knew so well declared she was very late for a hair appointment, the call was costing money, and she had to go. Now. So much for all that newfound sensitivity. Clearly, Greta G. had more work to do if she wanted to bring out more good from her producer.

As complex as problems sometimes seem to be, a good toss and a good meal can work wonders.

It's Sophisticated, It's Complex, but It's As Easy As Flicking a Switch

It may sound simplistic to say that the Magic Touch throwing technique will solve many of the problems you're having with your dog or your cat. But it will.

Our lives have become so programmed, so expensive, so mind-crunchingly confusing and complex, so controlled by marketing and opinion polls, so overtaxed, so overstressed, and so difficult, that something so simple in its execution and theory could work so completely, effectively, and so quickly is hard for our frazzled brains to accept straightaway. Well, accept it, it works.

It does sound too good to be true sometimes. The two-legged, book-reading, moviegoing, television-watching species, with all of his documented smarts, has become skeptical and jaded along the path of progress, and something that is easy to do, that doesn't cost anything, any money, how can it really work? Well, skeptical or not, when tried, it's true.

The Magic Touch is actually a sophisticated technique. This philosophy immediately sets into operation many factors working all at once—your throwing, your dog or cat's sense of smell, your new powerful standing in their eyes, the ability to reach them at a distance. They are not primates, not built to throw, and they will never figure out how you can do this, will never be able to neutralize this new ability of yours.

It's sophisticated and at the same time quite simple. It's complexity reduced to its most common denominator, which is common sense. Let's put it this way: you flick a switch and there is light. This is easy for you to do and you don't have to think about it. If you did think about it, all the science that went into this simple action, to give you the benefit of light, you would see that it is actually a complex chain of events. This simple light switch sets into motion many intricate, electrical principles and physical properties that make it work.

Simply put, the answers that you've been given to solve problems, the bill of goods you've been sold up until now, will not work. They are not real answers to real problems, they are only complex forms of double-talk, they do not take into consideration your animal's supersenses and intelligence. They're only Band-Aids and excuses, and once they are removed, the problems will remain or even get worse.

You can never compete with your dog's and cat's senses or physical abilities, which are so much more developed than yours. They can see better, hear better, smell better, run faster, and jump higher than you; pound for pound you are outclassed. You are out of the game. So, what you *can* do, to turn this situation around, is to use our Magic Touch. With it, you are back in the game. You will become the coach the players look up to, you will become powerful and awesome in the eyes of your dog and cat. Without the Touch side of our triangle, you could be looking for the ballpark forever and never find the diamond.

Shadow's List

1. Barking when I went out.
2. Not coming when called.
3. Won't walk on a leash without pulling or constantly stopping.
4. Staying.
5. Picks up anything, anywhere.
6. When I'm not paying attention to him, he would become destructive.
7. Barks in the morning when we're staying with friends or family.
8. Runs out of the apartment every time you open the door.
9. At home and at friends', forgot he was paper-trained.

August 31, 1998

Dear Paul and Suzie:

I just wanted to tell you how much happier Shadow and I are. I love being the "leader of the pack." I don't know if I told you, but you were my fourth trainer for a 13-month, 4.5-lb. Yorkie, who is extremely smart and stubborn. When you told me Shadow would come to me forever and always after one half hour of training and he would stop running in the hall every time I opened the door, I was very skeptical, but you did it.

I'm no longer screaming at the top of my lungs to try to get Shadow to do what he is supposed to do or begging him to come while I'm offering him cookies. My friends who have seen him just sit here with their mouths open. When we're out at the beach, he walks with me without a leash. In the city, he is no longer pulling and choking himself. He even went to the movies with me (in his bag, of course).

In addition to your great training, your follow-up has been terrific and I feel you are here keeping an eye on us. One of the things you said to me on the phone before we met was "the dog should fit into my life, not me into his, and his training should be during daily events not just a training session." This is one of the best parts of your philosophy.

You'll never know just how happy you've made me . . . I was at the point of seriously considering giving Shadow away and now I would never consider it.

> *Sincerely,*
> *Joan and Shadow*
> *NYC*

Note: For those interested in doppelgängers and Schrödinger's hypothetical quantum cat, who may have had many lives and all at the same time, read Malcolm W. Browne's article in the *New York Times*, May 28, 1996, "Physicists Put Atom in 2 Places at Once."

CHAPTER 6

Element Two: Diet

To Eat or Not to Eat—What Is the Question?
There's nothing like the real thing.

February 25, 1998

Dear Paul and Suzanne,

After one month of following your regime of "no dry dog food," Hadley's bloodshot, draining eyes have subsided—he no longer has the dry, encrusted patches of skin that he constantly chewed and scratched. His coat is healthy and shiny and his fur is growing back over his bald spots!

Many, many thanks for all your commonsense *advice and recommendations.*

Hope you enjoy the enclosed fruit-slice candies from our factory. Hadley does!

Sincerely,
Nancy K. and Hadley
Massachusetts

Our "commonsense advice and recommendations" were to take Hadley off all his dry dog food and related dry-food products, including biscuits and rawhides. By changing Hadley's diet to one of good fresh food, we were then able to stop all of the medication he was being subjected to, including steroids for his bloodshot, draining eyes and massive skin problems. He had been pumped full of these steroids for two years, along with thyroid medication he was being given for a "nonspecific" thyroid condition.

Hadley became a new man in both mind and body. He got back the looks and energy that a five-year-old blond cocker spaniel should have. He runs and plays like a teenager and has now become an ardent swimmer, loving to dive and bodysurf in the ocean.

The Postman

"Neither snow, nor rain, nor heat, nor gloom of night stays these couriers from the swift completion of their appointed rounds."

He took a couple of real good gulps of water; he wanted to make sure he had enough to sustain him when he went out on patrol. He couldn't be sure how long he'd be out patrolling, and he needed to have enough water in him to complete his appointed rounds.

He would be sure to make certain that his domain was fully secure and well pissed on. He wanted anyone coming into it, any trespassers on his turf, to know, in no uncertain terms, that this land was his land, and his land alone. Those who thought differently would be in big trouble if they dared try to move in, or even if no one came. This was the Postman's personal postmark, his grand signature, a spotted carpets policy. Watermarks, for one and all to see, smell, or step in.

The Postman, methodically and patiently visited every quadrant of space, took a three-legged stance, and squirted his ownership with utter determination.

This Postman is Vito Postman, a fiery little Italian greyhound, belonging to Randall Postman, who is very upset that his Vito is peeing and pooping all over the house. Randall is dog tired of picking up all of Vito's deliveries. Not one of which was ever delivered at the proper time or to the proper address. Randall was also upset by the odor that permeated from these numerous unwelcome deliveries. Vito on the other hand was quite happy with his grand movements and his *parfum*, eau d'Vito.

Changing from dry dog food to an exciting diet of fresh food cut Vito's pee and poop volume down by half. A good, well-placed, loving slap on the behind took care of the rest of Randall Postman's Vito headaches. Now Vito Postman delivers on time, when and where he's supposed to.

Diet: The Right Stuff

The second element of our triangle is proper diet. Think about this. Why are cancers and tumors in dogs and cats on the rise? They are. (Source: Veterinary medical database at Purdue University, search date 1/30/98.) We know that dogs and cats don't smoke cigarettes. We know that dogs and cats don't drink alcohol. We certainly know that dogs and cats don't take their coats off and bask in the sun. And another thing we do know is that the most popular dog and cat food in this country is the dry kind.

We understand that environmental factors play a part in all of this; of course they do. However, a most important factor, and the one we consider the most important factor for good health, is good food, healthy food, and a well-balanced, varied, proper diet.

What you eat and how you treat your body is paramount to your health and well-being. As the saying goes, "You are what you eat." This is not exclusive to the human-species, elite social club. This is true for all social clubs of any species.

All foods, after fresh food, we consider substitutes for fresh food. Canned foods, frozen foods, or cereals are not bad, and they are convenient, but you could justifiably argue that fresh meats, fresh fish, fresh vegetables, fresh fruits, and fresh-made breads are more nutritious and delicious than their canned, frozen, or dried-out mysterious, distant cousins.

For one thing, you know exactly what is in fresh. Many substitute foods, processed foods, have other things added along with the food—flavor enhancers, supplements, chemicals, colorings, preservatives—to keep them from spoiling and give them a long shelf life and an acceptable taste.

The quality of the commercial food that dogs and cats eat is not even as good as the substitute, processed foods humans eat. According to the Food and Drug Administration, most dog and cat food is made from stuff that's not fit for human consumption.

Dog and cat food, on its way to the can or bag, has also gone through a rendering process, a couple of steps down from common processing.

It's no secret that good sex and good food are two of the greatest pleasures in life. We're not going to discuss sex in this book, or maybe we will, but we will talk about that other great pleasure, good food, good-tasting food, and the right kind of food. Food that is good for health as well as pleasure.

By the way, variety is said to be the spice of life. What variety can you possibly give your dog or cat with a pet food? None. Unless the company's name is Variety pet foods.

Total Confusion

In the human world, the abundant information about diet can make it confusing to know what and when to eat.

There are the high-protein diets and the low-protein diets, the vegetarian diets, the Mediterranean diets, the serotonin-level diets, and the macrobiotic diets, to name a few. All of these diets have merit, but it can take a lot of time and energy to follow these regimens continuously. Many people get tired of being told what to eat, especially if the food doesn't taste all that good at times.

There is advice to eat three meals a day, the advice to eat six small meals a day, don't eat at all from time to time, fast once a week, or maybe you're better off drinking special shakes, colorful powders, or eating power bars instead of food. This advice also has merit, if you can figure it out, but also becomes difficult to follow rigorously.

Then you're warned, don't eat processed, refined white flours or sugars. Complex carbohydrates such as whole-grain breads, brown rice, cereals, and potatoes are much better for you. You are cautioned that even eating too much fruit can be bad because fruit has a lot of sugar, for the sugar-sensitive ones, those with the elevator-type, going-up-or-going-down blood sugar levels.

If that's not enough, there's also the health-food advisory to not eat anything but organic, if you can get it; eat only free-range, get meats without antibiotics or steroids, and then there are the new instructions to follow for disinfecting your kitchen and yourself after handling and cooking different foods. It makes you just want to give up eating altogether.

Oils, such as palm and cottonseed, and also partially hydrogenated, chemically altered ones, such as margarine and other transfatty acids, you are told to avoid like the plague. You're advised to use primarily olive and canola oil, and if you must use butter, eat it in small amounts. And then there is flaxseed oil. It's good for you but it falls into the same category as cod-liver oil—yuck! We have to fight to get a tablespoon of it down in the morning. Moms say, "Eat it and be quiet, it's good for you." Double yuck, mom. This oily, slippery slope also has merit.

By the way, you're not allowed to eat those french fries that you love so much because they could be fried up in the n.g. oils! Even though you might crave those french fries, resist. We must confess, from time to time we take our life in our hands and eat french fries; gotta have 'em, we love 'em.

We're told dairy products can clog arteries and can cause allergies, but on the other hand, it's suggested you take them for needed calcium. What to do? What to do?

Wheat, dairy, soy, corn, and yeast can be the culprits in allergy attacks. These attacks can be sudden and swift and hit without warning, by just inhaling the dust of any one of the above vectors of allergies.

It's gotten to the point where some are afraid to get within miles of certain foods because they've been frightened by media news that some food could be poisoned, tainted, or could carry weird bacteria along with it. And that's not to mention the scary water that comes temptingly out of the tap. Should you or shouldn't you drink it? Only a chemist knows for sure.

Many food mavens alert you to the power of food to change your behavior. Some foods can put you to sleep, some foods can cause anxiety attacks, some can help you get to Olympic stardom, some can even give you good grades in school.

According to some, certain foods might even make you kill. Even tiny, little Twinkies, with the unidentifiable delicious cream inside, came under vicious attack from all nutritional fronts and even the rears. Poor, tiny, little Twinkies, having to be dragged into court, to defend someone being accused of manslaughter. The defendant claimed the sugar in the cake made him crazy. "The sugar made me do it" defense wasn't successful.

How much salt will kill you, no one can agree on. How many

eggs are good, no one knows. Hopefully, if the eggs are organic, and from happy, healthy, free-range hens, they're okay, they won't kill you and will provide good protein.

They say, they say, these many, many, many experts, whoever these many may be, they say all of these things. Even a late, famous baby doctor before passing on to greener, organic pastures recommended that all children over the age of two should be vegetarians and avoid dairy products, including milk. If you like that, that's okay, too. But it takes a lot of work to balance that kind of a diet.

For those of you who love and depend on supplements, keep depending on them, they can't hurt, but don't use supplements in place of good food. That can hurt. Supplements supplement food, they are not food.

Quality Control

With the myriad of experts pulling and tugging and telling and screaming, and warning you what to eat and what not to eat, when to eat and how to eat and how not to eat, and with all the different foods available to eat, a couple of simple things we do know and that most seem to agree on is that the higher the quality of the food, the better. The less refined, the less processed, the more preservative and drug free, the better. Meaning, the fresher you can get your food, the better off you will be.

We enjoy going to different markets to shop, for ourselves and for our four-footed, furry friends and our two-legged, fine-feathered friends. And we don't mean that fella in the chicken costume, the one at the ball games, we don't know him. But we bet even this chicken dresser loves good food.

The same good-commonsense principle should also apply when feeding your dog and cat. Where in this spectrum of great-tasting, good, fresh food do you fit dry or canned dog or cat food? No matter how you try to pour it out, spoon it out, fit it in, squeeze it, process it, enhance it, dress it up, label it, talk about it, or market it, it doesn't fit in anywhere. It is a substitute for fresh food.

With an abundance of information and an abundance of good food around, why should you be left just holding the bag? Not even a vacuum-sealed, airtight bag at that. And then there's the can. It contains moisture and it's vacuum-packed. So what? These are substitute foods of rendered by-products not fit for human consumption. Most everything in the original food has been processed out or melted down, and then to meet your cat's and dog's minimum basic requirements, supplements have been added.

Rendering is "the ancient but seldom-discussed practice of boiling down and making feed meal and other products out of slaughterhouse and restaurant scraps, dead farm animals, road kill, and distasteful as it may seem—cats and dogs euthanized in some animal shelters.

". . . Renderers in the United States pick up 100 million pounds of waste material every day—a witch's brew of feet, heads, stomachs, intestines, hooves, spinal cords, tails, grease, feathers, and bones. Half of every butchered cow and a third of every pig is not consumed by humans. An estimated six million to seven million dogs and cats are killed in animal shelters each year, said Jeff Frace, a spokesman for the American Society for the Prevention of Cruelty to Animals in New York City.

"For example, the city of Los Angeles sends 200 tons of euthanized cats and dogs to West Coast Rendering, in Los Angeles, every month, according to Chuck Ellis, a spokesman for the city's Sanitation department.

"Pet food companies try not to buy meat and bone meal from renderers who grind up cats and dogs," said Doug Anderson, president of Darling International Inc., a large rendering company in Dallas. "We do not accept companion animals," he said. "But there are still a number of small plants that will render anything." (Sandra Blakeslee, "Fear of Disease Prompts New Look at Rendering," *New York Times*, March 11, 1997, C1.)

The *New York Times* continued its interviews with city officials and renderers. In the rendering process the waste material is "minced" and "steam cooked" and the lighter and heavier materials are separated. "The heavier protein material on the bottom goes through a separate process," Mr. Blanton said [executive director of the National Renderers Assoc.]. "It is dried, squeezed to remove more fat and dried again. The resulting powder is the major ingredient in pet and animal feed. It is a cannibalistic practice that has proved highly profitable." (Ibid.)

This is not exactly the *Joy of Cooking*, is it? What would you food purists, sensitive ones, and gonsa magillas have to say about all of this? Would you eat this stuff? This wonderful stew that the FDA, looking to protect you, says is not for you to eat? Where does this fit in, in our knowledge and experience of good food? If your dog or cat invited you to sit down for dinner with them and they were going to happily and generously share their wonderful dog and cat food, a pot-au-feu stew, with you, would you accept? Blaaaah . . .

This discussion also underlines the importance of having a well-behaved dog or cat, so that he doesn't end up as part of someone's dinner. This strikes us as the feline, canine Sweeney Todd meat-pie syndrome.

This doesn't mean that all pet food contains cannibalistic renderings, but who knows? Who's to say? A pet food company? A veterinarian? Who? What great detective is going to jump into that vat containing the millions of tons of dead animals to pluck out a stray dog or cat that might have been dropped in there by mistake?

Would it be a Poirot, a Holmes, or a Spade? Whoever this PI might be, he might have trouble wading through the millions of pounds of tainted chopped meat that was recalled from the human market and found a home in the pet food industry back in 1998. One of these famous sleuths might even become part of this "witch's brew," if he does not watch his step. How would you classify a missing detective as an ingredient of this brew? Would he be a crude protein? Would his clothes have any nutritional value? Maybe for fiber? Would his gun or flashlight be considered sources for trace elements of iron?

There seems to be no real control over the pet food industry other than that exercised by the companies themselves, sort of like the proverbial fox in the henhouse.

According to *Consumer Reports* ("Pet Food," February 1998), "The AAFCO is a nonprofit association of federal and state officials that develops guidelines for production, labeling, and sale of animal feed." This association has two established standards. One is in nutrient profiles and the other is in feeding trials. But both standards have shortcomings. "The nutrient profiles don't guarantee that a dog or cat will be able to absorb the needed nutrients in a food. Furthermore, the profiles are based on the best available knowledge of what nutrients dogs and cats need to stay healthy. Because that knowledge is not firm for all nutrients, the numbers are somewhat arbitrary." Feeding trials also have problems. "First, a feeding trial need take place for only six months for the food to claim it can maintain an adult animal's health. That may not be long enough for certain deficiencies to show up. Second, once a company has subjected a particular product to a feeding trial, it's allowed to put a feeding-trial statement on other products in the same 'family'—products that the company claims have similar nutrition. What's a family? AAFCO is trying to get the industry to agree on a definition; meanwhile, it's whatever a company wants it to be. Puppy foods, low-calorie diets, and adult dog foods can all claim to be nutritionally complete and balanced even when only one flavor of one product was subjected to a feeding trial. There's no way for consumers to know if the product they're buying is the one animals have thrived on, or only a distant relative."

In a nutshell, nobody is required to listen or adhere to anybody's standards except his own. If you really want something good, something balanced, and something you can identify from top to bottom, fresh food that you put together is the only food with a guaranteed analysis, and the ingredients can be as minimum or maximum as you want. And you will know for sure what's in there.

Trying to get understandable information and reliable information from these manufacturers of pet food seems to be like going on a quest to fight windmills, but at least Don Quixote could see the windmills he determined to vanquish in his impossible dream. In this case, you can't even find the windmills to dream about. They seem to be all around but impossible to touch. And when you ask for information about these windmills, you're told, "You don't need to know, they know best, they are the experts, they are the food professionals, so don't worry."

Try to get your brain around the question of the contents in a can of typical dog or cat food. It's a real piece of work. There's minimums and maximums, ifs, ands, and buts, and a few maybes all making their way around that gigantic windmill. These are all rounded out and covered over very nicely with approximates and stretchable percentages, and a lot of wind.

An Egg in the Pool

We were highly engrossed in and entertained by some reading material a pet food company had sent us regarding their food. We were so mesmerized by it that our eyes crossed and our brains started to cook; you could almost smell smoke. To put it more plainly, we were totally confused trying to decipher this cryptography, these coded messages, these labels, the ingredients and all their percentages.

We called a representative for help and clarification. We were trying to determine how much protein was truly in their canned food. For example, if a can has a minimum of 10 percent protein, how does this same amount become 40 percent? It was explained to us that when you remove the water, the protein percent becomes 40 percent in that same can. This is called the dry-weight analysis.

"The label on every food must carry a guaranteed analysis which shows a percentage of moisture (water) in the food. The percentages shown on a guaranteed analysis are 'minimums' and 'maximums' and ARE NOT the exact amounts found in the food. However, since the actual figures are usually not available, those on the guaranteed analysis offer the 'next best' alternative." ("Science Diet," the "dry weight" analysis faxed to us by Hills Consumer Affairs Department, August 24, 1998.)

This is how they figure it out. If you take the moisture out of the can, the 75 percent moisture, then divide the 10 percent protein by the remaining 25 percent dry matter, this will actually give you 40 percent protein, dry-weight analysis. Now your can doesn't have only 10 percent protein in it, it has 40 percent protein in the dry-weight analysis. Confused yet? It sounds like a slight case of prestidigitation to us.

Please, get those detectives out of that vat and get them down here at once, we need them, we need some heavy-duty, decisive detecting help.

All right, now that we have our thinking caps on, pen in one hand, calculator in the other, the game's afoot.

As far as we are concerned, a protein amount in grams, say

eight grams of protein, is always eight grams of protein no matter how much water you put on it. For example, a jumbo egg
has eight grams of protein. If you put this egg in a swimming
pool, that pool, with a thousand gallons of water, still has eight
grams of egg protein in it. Unless the bugs weren't filtered out
of the pool; in that case, figure in a bit of bug protein. When
you take the egg out of the pool, there is no protein in the pool,
except the bugs and unless you went in for a swim. Since we
don't know your weight, or the weight of the bugs, not even the
approximate percentages of all of you, we can't tell you how
much protein has now entered the pool.

Why all of the complicated puzzlement over an amount of
an ingredient in a food? In our human-elite-species social club,
food, any food that's labeled, the label clearly and simply tells
you what you want to know. What it is you are eating. It doesn't
say that if you really want to know what's in here, you have to
do scientific analysis or take your food to a lab. You know
what's in what you eat.

Coming now to your neighborhood fooderies will be new labels regarding irradiation of food. Should they or shouldn't
they say it, and how big should they say it? On dog and cat food
they're still saying what they want to say, one way or the other,
even if it's difficult for you to decipher.

Why is everything approximate? Why only minimum and
maximum? Why aren't the actual figures, "usually not available," available? Why are the figures on the guaranteed-
analysis ingredient labels only the "next best alternative"? A
guarantee is supposed to be just that, a guarantee.

Take the egg out of the pool, add a couple more, scramble
them in a little butter, with peppers and onions, add a couple
slices of tomato on the side, and *bon appétit*. Have a nice
breakfast, you and your dog or cat. Don't burn the toast.

For you more advanced breakfast makers, use the eggs for

French toast, use the eggs for a variety of pancakes or frittatas or soufflés. For you Continental types, you can make eggs Benedict, salmon Benedict, avocado Benedict, or spinach Benedict. As you can plainly see, there's more to an egg than putting it in a pool. And there's more to certain food labels than meets the eye, and possibly a lot less.

Quality Control

To us, fresh food is real food. The only food. It looks like food, it smells like food, it tastes good like food should taste, and it is loaded, chock-full of nutrition. That's what you feed your dog and cat. On the other hand, there is the other stuff. You be the judge and then you be the jury.

Balance Control

Balancing a diet for your dog or cat is quite simple, healthy, and economical when you think about it. The experts will try to profit by your confusion by convincing you that processed, dried-out food is better than fresh food. Step back and think about it.

Use our simple ingredient recommendations as your baseline guide and then you can feel free to vary your dog's or your cat's food along the lines of your personal likes and dislikes, and along the lines of the most important dietary requirement: "What's in the fridge, what's in the cupboard, what's for dinner?" Whatever you have in the house for yourself and your family. Our plan is not a rigid, inflexible one, it's one you'll be able to follow forever and gives full play to your creativity and imagination. And gives your dogs and cats the real spice of life, variety.

If you look on the ingredients breakdown of all dog and cat

foods, you'll see the main ingredients are usually, we hope (if you're lucky), chicken, beef, lamb, and rice, peppered with maybe some vegetables and a lot of by-products and supplements.

One can only watch in amazement a television commercial where the advertiser will try to convince you that the dried-out, colored pieces of something in their dry food is really peas and carrots! Maybe, but they were peas and carrots in another lifetime. These foods may or may not be balanced, and they may or may not meet the minimum daily nutrient requirements.

If you are going to feed your dog or cat processed chicken or beef, and this meat is not of the highest grade to begin with, and processed rice and vegetables, and these are not of the highest grade, and the food has a shelf life of who knows how long, and how long has that food been on the shelf in the first place, and what else is in this food to sustain its longevity and balance—why not just give your animals the good, healthy, fresh stuff?

Real fresh chicken, beef, seafood, vegetables, rice, beans, pasta, potatoes, cereal, bread, butter, apples, oranges, plums, cheese, and any other foods we left out that could be good—including french fries, from time to time. This list could go on and on. There's so much good food in the world, give it to your dog and cat.

No one should be able to convince you that a low-grade, low-quality, processed, canned, or dried-out piece of chicken is healthier for you, or for your dog or cat, than fresh chicken—roasted, broiled, baked, parmigiana, or for you spice lovers, *fra diavolo*.

Common sense should prevail. An identifiable, balanced diet of fresh food is better for dogs and cats than an unidentifiable, balanced diet of processed who knows what? With fresh food you know what's in it. With pet food you're told approximately what's in it. Why not just eat fresh food? It's fun and it's easy, and your dog and cat will love you for the good food and never think of leaving home, ever.

One-Third Protein, One-Third Carbohydrates, One-Third Steamed Vegetables

The argument that fresh food might not be "balanced" or that you are not capable of balancing a good diet for your dog or cat is ridiculous. Balancing a fresh-food diet for your dog and cat is a simple matter. One-third protein, one-third carbohydrates, and one-third steamed vegetables—that's a balanced, basic diet.

You can add more of whatever you want to. Whatever you have in the house. If the family is eating spaghetti marinara one night without a meat protein, then that's what your animals eat, too. They won't die. Few two-legged or four-legged animals ever get a perfectly balanced diet every day of their lives. Somehow they manage to stay alive and healthy until the next meal, and then some. However, to eat the same thing, day in and day out, for your whole life, could very well bore you to death. Think of your poor dog or cat eating the same old boring stuff, every day of his life.

Once in a while you just want to enjoy yourself and eat, maybe a slice of pizza or some Chinese dumplings or a nice piece of apple pie with some vanilla ice cream on it or even a little chocolate. As long as you don't overdo anything, you'll both be fine and happy.

For puppies, especially large or giant-breed puppies, because they grow so fast in their formative years, make sure you give them all they need, proper balanced foods, with good variety and lots of good nutrition. Our one-third, one-third, one-third works just fine. Even a growing puppy can miss a completely balanced meal once in a while and have a slice of pizza or a tuna-fish sandwich instead.

Conspiracy Theory

You now not only have control of what goes into your dog and cat, but just as important, you also know what it is. Otherwise, the only information you're going to get is from commercial, profit-making food companies and veterinarians, who also make a profit on the dog and cat foods they sell and who are dependent on these food companies for most of their nutritional information.

That would be like you listening to a food company, or your doctor telling you not to eat fresh food, that it's not as good as processed, canned, or dried-out food.

You cannot solely depend on the words of a few or on the massive blitz of advertising promises for all of your dog's or cat's nutritional information, just as you wouldn't depend solely on your doctor or a food company to tell you all you need to know about your health and nutrition.

By the way, when was the last time you went to your doctor and he pulled down a case of food for you to buy and take home? When was the last time your doctor made money out of the food he sold you out of his office?

"Hill's, Iams, and Eukanuba certainly benefit someone's bottom line: According to one estimate, vets who sell those foods directly from their offices can reap profits of up to 40 percent.

"Manufacturers justify higher prices by noting that their foods are made with the same ingredients, whatever their cost. On the other hand, producers of less expensive foods may vary the formula, to keep costs down, while claiming to maintain the required nutrient levels. Our tests confirmed that expensive foods tend to have more consistent nutrition, batch to batch, than inexpensive foods. Is that a real advantage? Maybe, but no research has shown that such consistency improves the food's quality or the pet's health." (*Consumer Reports*, "Pet Food," February 1998.) Based on research done by *Consumer Reports* as to the merits of superpremium foods or grocery-store foods, they report that they saw "no persuasive evidence that such foods keep pets healthier over the long term or help them live longer." (*Consumer Reports*, "Pet Food Update," May 1998.)

Any special foods you buy from a veterinarian are not as good as fresh food. Remember when veterinarians told you to give your dog and cat chicken and rice when your dog or cat got sick? Chicken and rice are still good for your dog or cat when they get sick. If your dog or cat is unable to eat solid food, chicken soup can't hoit. It sounds bizarre to us that a dog or a cat has to get sick before he can put a decent meal into his stomach.

And then there are those who make expensive gourmet pet foods. Chefs, please, just give the dog and the cat a good dinner from a gourmet people chef. He'll love you for it. Don't make gourmet doggy foods, just give your dog what you eat and love, and don't give them what you don't like to eat.

If a proper, healthy diet is so important to you, then why would you trust a dog food company and all of their consultants and marketing experts to give you all and the only information available about food for your best friends?

With dog food companies controlling the airwaves and with veterinarians controlling the professional "listen to ME's," it can almost be thought of as a major conspiracy, the food-conspiracy theory.

You can beat this, however, by just thinking things through, informing yourself, and asking lots of basic, commonsense questions, and *waiting* for the answers. Make sure you get answers, not an answer like "They've been working on diet and nutrition for so many years, they must know what they are do-ing." Hell, nobody knows everything. Especially those who claim they do. Remember, self-praise generally doesn't smell so good. It stinks.

Weight Control. Too Fat? Too Thin?

If you feel your cat or dog is getting heavy, cut back on the food. If you feel your dog or cat needs more food, add it. Every dog and cat has an individual metabolism and lifestyle.

If you are not certain if your dog or cat is gaining or losing weight, get a scale and get an accurate weight. Many of us, overwhelmed with fascination and obsessiveness about our own weight, can look at our dogs or cats with a distorted eye and a wink and a nod.

We can rationalize our weight numbers to a point of making the unwanted numbers not so unwanted. Don't trust your ea-gle eye to see this problem clearly; trust a good trusty scale, not an old, unused, rusty one.

In discussions about obesity and how to deal with it in cats and dogs, the experts will talk about getting these animals off any additional fresh-food "people" snacks that indulgent own-ers lovingly give them. The experts feel these snacks put the ex-tra, unwanted weight on. They don't talk about cutting back on pet food; if anything, they might tell you to purchase the diet pet foods for your dog and cat instead.

Their reasoning is, first of all, that it's not the dog and cat food that's getting the animal fat, it's all the other food, the "people food," that's doing it. And just to cover all the bases, buy a cou-ple of bags of the light pet food. This is a funny way to think. We see this reasoning like an adventure through the looking glass where everything is backward and upside down. Don't take away the good stuff, take away the other stuff.

Take these cats and dogs off pet foods, especially the dry kind, and you'll see pounds melt away, disappear before your very eyes like magic, without depriving them of the joy of eating. And at the same time, you'll know exactly how much food your dog and cat are getting. Then you can easily control their weight and health. Most of all, your dog and cat will relish the eating, the getting into and staying in shape, all at the same time.

Another reason your dog or cat could be overweight might be that late at night, when everyone is asleep, four furry feet hit the floor and pitter-patter quietly into the kitchen, open up the fridge, carefully remove the plastic wraps off the turkey or chicken left over from dinner, and eat it all up.

These midnight food raiders will then stack the dishes in the washer, throw out the garbage, and leave no clues or signs whatsoever that they had a paw in any crime. Or that any crime was committed. No one will ever suspect any fowl play. These raiders will then go back to sleep as if nothing had ever happened, except that they might be pleasantly plumper in the morning. If that's what's happening, put a lock on the fridge to stop them and an alarm on the fridge to warn you of a crime in progress.

But if you want to know for sure that hungry pets are on the prowl, then you might want to sprinkle a lot of print powder on the floor, and that should tell you exactly who the culprit is, because prints don't lie. If you see large prints with a big toe and a heel, sort of the kind that primates leave behind, it could be you, or the person sleeping next to you, prowling or sleepwalking for a midnight snack.

Cleans Teeth? There's Just No Way, José.

In addition to the concerns about balance, there is also the strange but pervasive idea that this dry and processed food has the ability to clean teeth. Well, just ask your own dentist if there is any food for you that can clean your teeth. The dentist might throw you out of the office, and there's your answer for your dog and cat. No food cleans teeth.

A toothbrush cleans teeth, a piece of gauze cleans teeth, a wet toweling cleans teeth. By the way, after you are thrown out of the dentist's office, being the dentist is a dentist, you are probably going to be charged for your visit. We know of no free dentists.

It's Fresh Food, Not People Food

Some like to call it people food, but all that is, is a way, for marketing reasons, to further separate the species and what they should eat. *Food is food is food.* Commercial companies want to make an alternative food, a separate food, a low-grade, low-performance energy food for pets. Don't buy into this.

For all those experts, including vets and dog and cat food companies, who say that dogs and cats shouldn't eat fresh food because the dogs or cats will get sick, and that fresh food could be harmful for them, we say that fresh food will be as good or bad for dogs and cats as it will be for people.

Fresh food can be harmful for people, dogs, and cats if it is poisoned. We don't think you would do this to a dog or to a cat or to a person. If you starve a dog, a cat, or a person, that's bad. If you put fresh food in a big box and then drop it on the head of a dog or a cat or a person, then that could be harmful, and painful.

Let's put an end to another fable. Your dog will not get diarrhea from fresh food. Your dog or cat might get diarrhea from eating too much food, too much of any kind of food, or food that's gone bad. They could get diarrhea from parasites, worms, or some medical condition. But diarrhea is not caused by fresh food alone.

Don't tell us that dog or cat food is better than fresh food, it never could be. Fresh is fresh, all the rest is an alternative.

Allergies and Skin Problems

Food is central to your animal's health, well-being, his behavior, and long life. We all agree, that's a given, without food he'll die. But you may not fully realize the impact of a good diet on your dog's or cat's health and well-being until you see an end to such problems as dry skin and coat, hot spots, lick granuloma, and allergies. These conditions clear up miraculously when you change their food to fresh.

You will get improvements in these health conditions by changing your furry friends' food from dry food to canned food, with no "pet treats," but supplemented with plenty of fresh-food treats.

But the real changes, the really big ones, happen when you go to fresh food *100 percent*.

Dogs and cats that eat a diet of strictly fresh food are the healthiest. This means not eating any of those pet food treats, including strange-treated bones, hides, ears, or hooves, or whatever else somebody dreams up that your dog or cat might love. You want to give a treat? Give them a treat that is good for them and that you would eat. Your barometer of what's okay goes this way. If it's good enough for you, it's good enough for them. If it's good enough for them, it's good enough for you.

Not only do the dog's or cat's skin and allergy problems rapidly clear up, but even people with allergies attributed to dogs and cats will not be allergic to these good-food eaters, ones that eat fresh food. This is across the board. Don't take our word for it, which is based on over forty-four years of experience. Try it yourself for a couple of weeks. The proof is in the pudding.

The improvements in the health of dogs and cats on fresh food are spectacular and dramatic. This simple fact that fresh food is really the best food that money can buy has either been dismissed, ignored, or overlooked. It should never have happened.

Thanksgiving Dinner

Isn't it a sad, sad comment that when you can sit down for Thanksgiving dinner, with all the good turkey, all the great stuffing and trimmings, cranberry sauce, and then for dessert stuff yourself further with pumpkin pie and ice cream, your dog or cat can't. Eating away to your heart's content, enjoying yourself with every mouthful, while your cat or dog is sitting somewhere nearby, looking at you, wanting some of that good stuff, and you, you look them right in the eye and say to them, "This food that I'm eating, and that I'm enjoying immensely, and that you can smell many times better than I can, is no good for you. It can only hurt you and make you sick and overweight.

"But, just to show you that I'm a real, real nice person, and in the holiday spirit, I'm going to go into the kitchen, under the sink, and take out a bag of that dry stuff—it says there's some turkey in it—and then I'm going to pour it into your special Thanksgiving dish. And I'm going to give you an extra Thanksgiving holiday present. I'm going to pour a few drops of turkey giblet gravy on it, not too much mind you, I don't want you to get sick, but just a few drops for taste, and I'm doing this just because I love you, and I'm a nice person and I know you'll just love it."

If cats and dogs could talk, we wonder what they would say to you, after you gave them all those few, good drops of Thanksgiving gravy. We don't think you'd want to know how they really feel about your holiday generosity and spirit.

If there ever were a water-muddying campaign, a conspiracy, a tragedy of Oedipal or edible proportions, it's got to be this one. The one that wants you to believe that the best and most nutritious food, fresh food, is really the worst, and that it is bad for your dogs and cats.

A small aside. An afterthought, an after-dinner mint, if you will, a tiny, thin mint. Now, with all of your dog's and cat's skin problems clearing up by making a simple dietary change, guess what? Putting dangerous steroids into your dog and cat will become a rarity, as well it should. Tell your vet to put that in his pipe and smoke it. If he doesn't smoke, offer him a couple of thin mints.

South of the Borderlines

Doctors insist that we not eat anything before a physical examination so that they can get an accurate reading of blood sugar, cholesterol, and any other readings from blood that are affected by eating. Therefore, why are cats and dogs given blood tests even if they've just had a major meal? Wouldn't this cause borderline changes in certain readings?

In the human world, doctors generally are not so quick to treat borderline results with medication. They do more testing or they send you for another opinion or you're observed for a time. Why are dogs and cats immediately treated for "borderline" or "nonspecific" conditions? Especially when these conditions many times clear up, all by themselves, with just a change of food.

We don't like to trespass into the veterinarian's domain,

because we are not veterinarians. However, in these cases of "borderline thyroid" and "borderline sugar problems" and "nonspecific readings" in dogs and cats, we've seen these "medical conditions" clear up as quickly as skin problems do with a change of food. So we feel it deserves to be mentioned.

If a vet is evaluating a thyroid condition, he will take other factors into consideration. Some of the criteria are bad skin, a dry coat, and if the dog or cat is lethargic. We don't want a bad coat, which could be caused by bad food, to be mistaken for a serious medical condition and then treated with steroids or other medications.

Changing the dog's or cat's food to fresh clears up the majority of these skin conditions. Good food is good medicine. It always has been and it always will be.

In the human world, proper diet plays a central role in the prevention, treatment, and cure of all kinds of illness. And so it should be when it comes to your dog or cat.

We received a press release recently from a veterinarian regarding a new food being put out by a well-known pet food company. Apparently they are developing a food to help "canine cancer patients." What's the magic bullet in this new food? They made the food taste better, so that the canine patients would like to eat it, and they added omega-3s and arginine. Omega-3s are found in fish oil, flaxseed oil, and cod-liver oil. Arginine, an amino acid, is found in meat, wheat germ, oats, peanuts, soybeans, and walnuts. (James F. Balch, M.D., and Phyllis A. Balch, C.N.C., *Prescription for Nutritional Healing* [New York: Avery, 1997], 36.)

What's the matter here? What's wrong with this picture? No one *can* cook for a sick dog? Or *should* cook for a sick dog? They must depend on a food company for a cure for a sick dog?

You want to give your dog a food he loves to eat, so that he will eat? Give him good fresh food; he'll eat. You want to give him omega-3s? Give him any fatty, oily fish to eat, such as salmon, which has thousands of milligrams of omega-3s, or cod-liver oil.

You want to help your dog or cat in the prevention of disease? Give him good fresh-food diets from day one. Why wait for your dog or cat to get sick before you give them a good meal of smoked salmon with omega-3 fatty acids?

You'll find that you and your dog and cat might be partial to a good Irish smoked salmon, Irish whole-grain brown bread, and a hefty slice of onion and tomato.

Or, maybe you and your dog and cat might go for a little bagel, cream cheese, Nova, onions, and capers, with a twist of lemon and a couple of black Greek olives on the side? Make sure you remove the pits from the olives.

Or, if your tastes run up to the Pacific Northwest cuisine, you might want your salmon fresh from the sea. A thick, boneless filet, smoked and herbed, over an open campfire, or maybe salmon carpaccio, along with some roasted garlic potatoes, and some steamed asparagus. All of these dishes, the salmon, the garlic, are strong health-guarding agents.

When you prepare fresh food for your dog and cat, you have the advantage of discovering and knowing what foods your animals will like the best. You will become their trusted chef extraordinaire.

If your dog or cat is ever recovering from an injury or an illness, then you will know which foods will best stimulate his interest and appetite. *Bon appétit*, to one and all.

These days good health (aka good food) is up to you. The more informed you are about food, vitamins and minerals, herbs, food combinations, and quality, the better off you and your family will be. Use your knowledge to help keep your dog and cat healthy, too. What's good for you is good for them.

Medications of any kind always carry their own set of side

effects and problems. How can you make certain of a right or true diagnosis and protect your dog or cat from being over-medicated? Ask lots of questions. Get a lot of answers. Get second opinions. Make sure your dog or cat doesn't eat before blood tests. Or, do what we do: many times we ask our own doctors for basic information. Read and research. You'll learn an awful lot.

Before going on the drugs, especially dangerous steroids for skin conditions, try changing your dog's or cat's food to fresh food. You might be pleasantly surprised that in a short time, a couple of weeks, the skin problems will disappear and you will have saved your dog or cat from a continuous cycle of these dangerous steroids, which can eventually harm your dog or cat permanently.

This is the steroid cycle: Skin problems equal steroids. They clear up. They come back. More steroids. They clear up. They come back. Meanwhile, the steroids are also working on the liver and kidneys. When does it end? When you stop steroids. That's when. When you change the food, that's when.

Fleas

On a fresh-food diet your dog's or cat's skin and coat will be rich and alive. Fleas will look for a drier landing field elsewhere. From time to time, you might find a flea or two. Just get rid of them. The way it's been done forever.

But your dog or cat won't be infested with fleas or need to wear a flea and tick collar or be subjected to poisons, inside or outside, to kill fleas and ticks. These poisons all say, "Keep out of the reach of children." That's for a reason. Why? Better yet, how is your child supposed to play with the dog or cat if the animal is wearing this poison, in any form, on any part of his body?

When dogs and cats are on fresh-food diets, their skin and coat will be rich and oily. Fleas and ticks, as a major problem, become moot. If you are using strong, medicated anti-flea-and-tick shampoos, you will dry the skin out. Use your own shampoo when you want to wash your dog or cat. We know you enjoy your shampoo. What's good for you is good for them.

Many human shampoos and other products are first tested on animals before they come to the marketplace for your use. Since these products have been tested on animals first, you might as well let them benefit from what they put their bodies and lives on the line for.

A Puddle Here, a Pile There, Obvious Damage Everywhere

If improving your dog's and cat's health and well-being with a food change isn't getting your attention, maybe all the positive changes in your home environment will.

You can put an end to housebreaking problems, destructive chewing, as well as ending the bad smells, the pungent, odoriferous perfumes that seep throughout your home. That no amount of room freshener can cover up. You know the ones we mean, the ones that remind you and all who enter that you have a cat or a dog.

With a proper diet, the strong body odor on your dog or cat will be gone for good, as well as that endless scratching.

When you change their food, the horizon will look and smell much brighter. No training necessary.

Behavioral Problems

Did you know that a large percentage of your pet's behavioral problems, including destructive chewing, and lousy, indiscriminate toilet habits, will end just with a change of diet? No training necessary.

Think about this. If you had to get to the bathroom and you couldn't, for whatever reason, you would be uncomfortable and nervous. You might chew your nails, pace, and fidget. If your dog has to get to the bathroom and he can't because he's been taught to hold and to wait until you take him out, and you're not always punctual with him, he'll also become a nervous wreck. He might just chew his nails, if you are lucky, but for sure he'll chew your house down.

Dry food makes your dog drink a lot of water. Drinking a lot of water means going to the bathroom a lot. The food expands in his stomach and he has to get to the toilet. Real bad. Getting to the toilet is a strong urge. Not even Superman can hold this need in for long.

You will easily be able to stop destructive chewing and have an easier time housebreaking your dog once you change the quality and amounts of food he is getting.

Table Manners

Your dog and cat will not become beggars or go wildly and madly out of control around food once you give them a fresh-food diet. You teach your animals table manners, and not to beg. You don't want to deny them a good meal.

If you invite friends over for dinner and your friends start jumping all over your dinner table, knocking food and plates over, begging and grabbing food, either you would physically throw them out of your house, ask them politely to leave, or call the police if they didn't listen. But most certainly you would not invite them back.

In the case of your dog or cat there is an easier solution. Just use the Magic Touch throw technique if they are at a distance, or a good, well-placed loving slap if they are within arm's reach, and tell them at the same time to behave themselves. It works. Remember, if it doesn't stop them the first time, do it a second time and a third time. When it stops, and it will, tell them how good they are and take a piece of the best food off the table and give it to them. Let them know they can have everything, when they behave. It is not confusing to them, they are smart.

We had lunch with a foreign diplomat, three of his guests, and his two favorite large Rhodesian Ridgeback dogs. This lunch was an elegant affair with white tablecloths, several exotic courses, and served up by experienced help.

The dogs weren't stupid. They decided to go as far away from their diplomat and us as possible. That meant bothering a guest at the farthest end of the table. They felt that person was the easiest mark for their wants and needs. They were right, they got everything from him. And had they kept pushing, they might have gotten all of his clothes and money as well.

Our diplomat, educated in the way of our Magic Touch, instinctively took his sneaker off and threw it down to the end of the table, missing his guest by a hair, catching the end of the table, knocking his beer off the table, but getting the dogs.

The dogs and the guest stopped interacting immediately. The guest went to the bathroom to clean up, and to get the beer off his pants. The dogs quickly came over to their diplomat and settled down near him. He smiled and gave them each a portion of his Moroccan chicken, couscous, and vegetables and then some cucumber-and-tomato salad.

The guest at the end of the table came back and, although smelling a bit from beer, was now able to eat the rest of his meal in peace.

The moral of this story is, be sensitive and understanding to your guests, even when telling your dogs to stop being pests. . . .

Dogs and cats, once they eat the same good food that you're eating, don't have to go crazy for food. Why would they? They know they are having what you're having. So they relax. The only time a person, a cat, or a dog becomes grabby and greedy is when he wants something that he can't have, but he sees everyone else having it. It's human nature.

In any case, whether it's just your dogs and cats bothering one guest, or many guests, or your guests bothering your dogs and cats, or dogs begging from everybody, or guests begging for attention from the dogs and cats, and everyone else, and trying to bribe them for their own reasons, whatever the combinations are, it's still your dinner table, it's your dinner, and you set the rules. Unless you don't want to.

But if you do, all you have to do at your table, no matter how many wild and unruly beggars arrive for dinner, of any species, if they come out of the woodwork, if they drop down from the ceiling, if they come by osmosis, no matter how the beggars arrive and no matter how many beggars arrive, the Magic Touch will keep order at your dining room table. It works.

If wishes were horses, then beggars would ride,
I'm overrun by the hordes, in anger she cried,
They're willful, they're wild, they're very hungry, you see,
But why, oh why, do they have to all eat dinner on me?

Wherever you like to eat, at the table, on the table, or even under the table, let your cats and dogs join you, as long as they listen to you. Teach them the manners that Emily Post, or any other manners maven, would approve of.

Making the Switch

We have convinced you to make the change from dry food to fresh food or canned food. How do you make this switch? You're told to wean your dog or cat slowly off one food and gradually introduce him to a new food.

Don't bother with this weaning procedure. Just throw out the old stuff and bring in the new. The only rule you have to follow is this: Give half the amount of food that would normally be given for one day. After that one day, give the normal amounts of food.

For example, if your dog or cat would normally eat 14 oz. of food, for one day give him 7 oz. And then go to your normal amount of 14 oz. the next day. That's it. It generally takes about twenty-four hours for your dog or cat to clean out his system and stop the need for drinking all that water.

Once your dog or cat is eating fresh food, you can vary his menu. If you have Italian food one night and you want some French food the next, you don't have to gradually wean yourself from one food to another, you just eat it. The same principle goes for your dog and cat.

If you are giving your dog or cat a canned-food diet, make sure to supplement this diet with lots of fresh-food snacks. And we mean lots of them, and we mean fresh.

A Change for the Better

Anthony and his friend Jim have a beautiful boxer puppy, Wilhemina, who is now about seven months old. They also have two other dogs in their family, and everyone eats a diet of good fresh food.

It wasn't always like this. Anthony and his friend had always given "the best canned dog food money could buy" to their two

Yorkshire terriers. They had been led to believe that this was the best food for them. They were wrong. The older of the two Yorkies, a female, eleven years old, had for a long time lost her appetite. She wouldn't eat no matter what they tried. She would even back away from her food.

At first they thought it was the bowl so they changed that. That didn't work. They had to hand-feed this little dog to get her to eat anything at all, to keep her alive. The other Yorkie, a male of ten years, had such bad breath that you never wanted to go near him. Halitosis personified. This bad-breath breather was "intolerable."

Wilhemina was on a fresh-food diet from day one, from the very first day that she joined this family. And from that very first day, so did all of the other four-footed, furry family members eat good fresh food.

Anthony remarked that switching to fresh food for all changed things dramatically for the better. The dogs all love their new food, especially the eleven-year-old. She is always happy to eat now, can't wait to eat, eats all of her food in record time and jumps into the food line for more.

The other Yorkie, the ten-year-old male, who used to have "intolerable bad breath," no longer has this socially embarrassing problem. His breath is now kissing sweet. In fact, there is no longer any dog smell in this house. And the change in the coats of all these dogs, especially of the two older ones, is "remarkable."

We're happy to know that Anthony's two Yorkshire terriers, now in their more senior years, are having a good time indulging in one of the great pleasures in life, eating, and eating well.

Element Two: Diet

MENUS

Anthony and Jim's Menu

All served in a proportion of ⅓, ⅓, ⅓

Monday, Tuesday, Wednesday
Broiled ground beef (not the leanest, Anthony wants the fat for taste), brown rice, peas, kidney beans, and chickpeas

Thursday, Friday, Saturday
Broiled chicken with pasta and any green vegetable—broccoli, peas, asparagus

Sunday, Monday, Tuesday
Liver, new potatoes, and vegetables—green, yellow, and orange (light on the carrots)

Wednesday, Thursday, Friday
Broiled ground beef, pasta, and vegetables

Snacks
A little cereal in the morning, leftovers of any kind, Stella D'oro biscuits (the dogs love them), and watermelon (the dogs are crazy for watermelon)

Eden and Mason's Menu for Higgens and Ms. Emma

Higgens is a five-year-old mini-poodle who has been happily raised on fresh food from the beginning, and Ms. Emma, a new addition to the family, is a standard-poodle puppy twenty weeks old and still growing healthily and happily. As you can see, the dogs get wide choices of what to eat for breakfast, lunch, dinner, and snacks.

THE HEART OF THE MATTER

Breakfast

Chicken, broccoli, brown rice

Oatmeal with butter and cinnamon

English muffin and egg

Emma loves Wheaties and milk

Whole-wheat pancakes, with a small amount of maple syrup

French toast

Smoked salmon and eggs and bagel with cream cheese

Dinner

Liver, onions, and rice

Ground beef, spaghetti, and broccoli

Turkey and chicken

Macaroni and cheese

Duck à l'orange with broccoli and rice—the dogs love this, who wouldn't?

Snacks

People animal crackers

Whole-wheat, whole-grain bread from bakery, and croissants with butter

Cheddar cheese and Jarlsberg (dogs don't go much for provolone)

Any kind of sweet fresh fruit (cut up): apples, cantaloupe, honeydew, grapes

Bananas

All dried fruits, such as pears and apricots

Vegetable chips—sweet potato and taro

Soy cheese and soy flour

Flat onion-bread crackers

Higgens loves wheat germ

Raw broccoli sprinkled with some olive oil, salt, and pepper

Myrna's Menu

Myrna and Lee have two grown-up cats, Purr and Peanuts, who love fresh asparagus, prepared in many different ways, sometimes steamed, sometimes with a butter sauce, so they get plenty, all they can eat.

Myrna also prepares cod or talapia. This fish is steamed with peas in a microwave and then cut up into small, bite-size pieces and is served along with a buttered baked potato. Purr and Peanuts also get turkey burgers, veggie burgers, and tuna-fish salad. They prefer tuna packed in water, not oil. Before bedtime, and as a snack, an occasional slice of kosher salami.

These cats have beautiful, shiny coats and are as happy as a couple of clams. When they want to, the cats also sit on chairs at the table with Myrna and Lee and get a smorgasbord of left-overs.

October 29, 1997

Dear Paul and Suzanne,

You saved my dog's life.

Willow, my dalmatian, had developed some frightening aggressive behavior. No more the engaging puppy, at age two, Willow could be dangerous. We needed help—fast. Although I'd read many books and we had taken traditional training classes (passing both beginner and intermediate levels) and had met with a private trainer—nothing had worked.

Willow, in spite of her problems, was still my precious dog, but nobody had a solution for us. I was desperate.

Then, it was our good fortune to find you two. With compassion and true understanding you were able to put me in control of my dog. The results were immediate and astonishing.

Willow now behaves well. She listens to me and does what is expected of her. She comes when called (always!) and stays close when off lead. Willow is a good dog—sweet, loving, friendly, contented.

Also, encouraged by both of you to discontinue dry dog food and to feed Willow fresh food—chicken, fish, veggies, potatoes, etc.—she became calmer. Then, as summers came and went, the large areas of itchy, red, bald skin irritations she would get from bug bites began to diminish until one summer, with no bug deterrent remedies given—internal or external—there were no skin problems at all. The diet of fresh, wholesome food was the cure.

Loeb and Hlavacek—you're the best!

Thanks once again,
Elizabeth and Willow, NYC

For those of you who say that you don't know how to cook, learn. For those of you who say you haven't time to cook, make time. For those of you who always eat out or order in, order a little more for your dogs and cats.

It's healthier for you and your dog and cat if you do take the time to learn about food and learn to cook. Remember, caring well for the Soul Mirror will help you care well for yourself. Looking at them is taking a good look at yourself.

NEW FOOD CHART

Vary amounts according to your dog's individual needs. Use your common sense. Everyone is a little bit different.

Using a 16 oz. measuring cup, fill one-third of it with protein: that's fish, meat, or chicken; one-third with carbohydrates: that's pasta, potatoes, rice, bread; and the last one-third with steamed vegetables: that's carrots, spinach, peas, broccoli, zucchini, lettuce, green pepper, tomato, or whatever other fresh vegetables are available.

- All dogs, big or small, short or tall, senior or junior, get a snack in the morning, something for breakfast. Whatever you're having, give them some.
- Snacks should be given all day.
- Canned food. If you want to feed your dog or cat canned food, use the equivalent of 16 oz. Add more food if needed, subtract if too much. Always supplement with fresh food.

Cats

Cats can and do eat vegetables. At the beginning you may have to blend the vegetables and carbohydrates into the food so that your cat won't pick them out. You'll soon notice that your cat will eat his vegetables and even look forward to them. For amounts, follow size chart below. For example, if your cat weighs in at ten pounds he would get up to one-half of a 16 oz. measuring cup or 7 to 8 oz. of food. This 7 to 8 oz. you can split up into two feedings. You can give your cat snacks all day. If your cat is too thin on this amount of food, add. If your cat is getting heavy on this amount of food, then cut back.

Free-Feeding a Large Breed Puppy

Because of their accelerated growth rate, large and giant breed puppies may need more food. If your puppy needs more food, you can start a midday meal and lots of snacks through-out the day. This should give him the food he needs to grow. If our chart is working for your puppy, then you don't have to add more meals, but don't stop his snacks.

At around six to nine months start cutting the food amounts down. If you've been giving your puppy lots of food, you may notice that at this age his voracious appetite is starting to level off. You can see if your puppy needs more or less food. You have to be the judge of this.

Puppies are just like growing children. They seem to be able to eat and eat and eat and never get fat. Then one day, voilà, it happens, they're too fat. You might recall, looking back over the years, how it was in your own life, that long time ago.

Every dog, every cat, and every person has a somewhat different metabolism; we all burn off the calories at different rates of speed.

Size Chart

Small—up to 15 lbs.
Medium—up to 45 lbs.
Medium large—up to 65 lbs.
Large to giant—up and up and away

Adult Dog: One Year and Up, Using a 16 oz. Measuring Cup
For 5 lb. dog up to ¼ of 16 oz. once a day

For 10 lb.	"	½	"	"
For 15 lb.	"	¾	"	"
For 20 lb.	"	1	"	"
For 50 lb.	"	2	"	"
For 100 lb.	"	4	"	2 in the morning, 2 in the evening

For dogs over 100 lbs. add accordingly

Guidelines for a Puppy

Use adult dog chart above for all weights and amounts.

Up to 4½ Months

Small dogs: TWICE a day, morning and evening.

Medium dogs: TWICE a day, morning and evening.

Medium large dogs: TWICE a day, morning and evening.

Large to giant dogs: TWICE a day, morning and evening.

Example: If your puppy weighs ten pounds, feed him the amount for a ten-pound *adult dog* TWICE a day. Once in the morning and again for his evening meal.

4½ Months to 6 Months

Small dogs: DECREASE morning meal by ½. Evening meal follow adult chart.

Medium dogs: DECREASE morning meal by ½. Evening meal follow adult chart.

Medium large dogs: DON'T DECREASE morning meal. Evening meal follow adult chart.

Large to giant dogs: DON'T DECREASE morning meal. Evening meal follow adult chart.

Example: If your 4½-month-old puppy weighs ten pounds, he now gets up to ¼ of 16 oz. in the morning and up to ½ of 16 oz. in the evening.

6 Months to 9 Months

Small dogs: One meal a day in evening. Follow adult chart for amount.

Medium dogs: DECREASE morning meal again by ½. Evening meal follow adult chart.

Medium large dogs: DON'T DECREASE morning meal. Evening meal follow adult chart.

Large to giant dogs: DON'T DECREASE morning meal. Evening meal follow adult chart.

9 Months to One Year

Medium dogs: One meal a day, if your dog looks good and is holding his weight. Evening meal follows adult chart.

Medium large dogs: DECREASE morning meal by ¼ to ½. Evening meal follow adult chart.

Large to giant dogs: DON'T DECREASE morning meal. Stay on two meals a day forever. Follow adult chart. For these large and giant dogs, don't feed more than three 16 oz. measuring cups at any one meal. If more food is necessary, start an afternoon meal.

In the final analysis you have to be the judge of how much food your dog and cat should have, and how they should look. Some people like their dogs slim, some like their dogs a little plumper. As long as they are healthy and happy, that's okay.

The food chart is a good one. It will help you with your feeding concerns. The food we recommend, fresh food, is the best food for your cats and dogs. You have to adjust the amounts of food to suit yourself and your furry friends, the same way you do for yourself.

Many people don't want to be bothered with calculating exact measures, so they just eyeball everything. They look at their dog and cat and guesstimate how much food they should have, and that's what they give them. That's okay as long as it's working. No one should argue with success.

If you are giving your dog or cat tons of good food snacks all day, which could add up to meals, adjust their main meals accordingly.

Some food experts will, for the human animal, advise eating six small meals a day instead of two or three large meals a day.

If this fits your lifestyle and you and your dog or cat like eating this way, then by all means go ahead. Referring back to the beginning of this chapter, and all of the expert dietary advisories, take the information that benefits you, including french fries, and follow that.

Remember what's good for you is good for your animals, as long as it is good and healthy. Nothing is written in stone and you are bound by no one but yourself.

Don't feed your cat and dog raw meats. There was a time when you could indulge in a delicious steak tartare. But now if you indulge in one of these raw eatings, it could very well bite you back in the form of E. coli, tapeworm, salmonella, or some other animal's revenge. Sushi, if you're having some, seems to be okay, so far. Who knows what the food mavens might say in the future?

Dogs and cats have been around long before dog and cat food companies and long before there were veterinarians and animal experts.

Some even think, now, that dogs could have been domesticated as long as 135,000 years ago. (Nicholas Wade, "Man Has Older Friend Than Thought," New York Times, June 13, 1997, A12.)

And when these good old friends, hominid and dog, gathered around their campfires at night, to talk about the day's events and experiences, did they also theorize and philosophize about the behavior and peculiarities of the other carnivores, herbivores, and omnivores, both big and small, that prowled the land? Did they discuss what these beings ate? Did they discuss the intelligence of these other creatures, whether these other creatures had the ability to reason or whether they functioned on pure "fight or flight" instinct?

And what about their feelings and emotions? Did these ancient animals have a wide range of emotions including empathy? Early man, woman, and dog probably talked late into the night on these topics; maybe they argued over which species was superior?

Some of these early animal behaviorists, way before Darwin, could have had anthropomorphic leanings. We'll never know.

Without a Judeo-Christian tradition way back then, who gave whom the role of domination over whom? Things were different back then. Were they more equal? Whose language was more developed? We'll never know the answer to these questions. One thing we do know about these campfire chitchats: they weren't eating any processed dog food, especially the dry kind. It's nowhere in evidence. It's never been found in the fossil record, to date.

And way back then, there were no veterinarians or pet food companies either; these experts didn't exist. They weren't anywhere to be found. There are no fossils of them in the records of time. Maybe because ancient hominids had no money to spend yet. These highly trained experts weren't around to tell ancient man and woman what to feed their dog. They weren't around to prescribe for early dog Prozac, steroids, or Valium as cure-alls, for all what ailed them, including psychological, behavioral, and skin problems. These problems didn't exist either, because there were no experts to diagnose them.

Experts weren't around with their miracle drugs and their miracle foods to give to the dogs who were chewing, who were destructive, who weren't housebroken, who made much too much noise, who were overweight, and who were stressed-out and suffering from the classic Acute Separation Anxiety Complex Syndrome.

Here's to the good old days, good old friends, and good old fireside chitchats, gone by.

As for the mysterious and elusive cats, we know they were revered much later in Egypt, but could it be that the cats watched the ancients socializing with their dogs, liked what they saw, made pilgrimages to Egypt, shrunk themselves down, and cuddled up to those in power? Those sly, mysterious, elusive, shape-changing cats.

Dogs and cats have been around a long, long time, way before expert food and expert opinion evolved. If you feed your cats and dogs a diet of good fresh food, they'll hang out by the campfire with you forever. They'll never want to leave.

CHAPTER 7

Element Three: You

Tracking the Tall Tales

Some are tall, some are small,
Some just make no sense at all.
Some are straight, some are crooked,
Some are used to get you snookered.

Plato's Retreat

Plato's philosophical and private dialogues on cage and crate confinement, whatever else strikes his fancy, and the nature of reality.

"The dog, is a cave animal. 'It' loves living in caves. That's why 'it' can be happy and secure living in 'its' very own

cave/crate/cage forever, if necessary. We might even call this crate/cage a 'condominium' for dogs."
—Many experts in USA, circa late twentieth century

The cave/crate/cage was rectangular in shape; it was two and a half feet long, two feet wide, and with its ceiling height of two feet, it towered above the floor. There was just enough room for the "cave dog" to stand up, and with a little squeeze here and a little squeeze there, he was able to turn around in it, too.

There were two small openings high up on either side of the crate, and one larger opening in the front. These openings were crisscrossed with a heavy wire. These small, crossed-wire openings gave the "cave dog" a limited field of vision, making it difficult for him to see much of the world around him.

Inside the crate it was always dark. Not much light could filter through those small barred openings and not much did. What little light did get in, formed shadow images on the interior walls of the crate, images of moving parts of the outside world. These shadow images all had crisscross patterns, as if they had been grilled on a barbecue.

What he saw through the limited openings of his "crate/cave" were bits and pieces of the outside world. He sometimes saw a section of a couch, sometimes parts of a plant, sometimes plates or containers of great-smelling food floated by, sometimes he saw a moving arm or a leg, and sometimes a head would appear in the distance, or some other body part, but he never saw a complete package or picture of anything.

Any sounds or voices that came into the crate were muffled ones, making it difficult to make sense out of any conversations, especially when they were always over your head and usually distant. What got through those wired holes in his crate were just the echoes of voices and background noise.

In his present situation, it was difficult for him to determine what was real and what was not. The nature of reality was twisted—no, it was crisscrossed. But he would sort it out. Isolated, he had plenty of meditation time.

The incarcerated tenant, forced to live in this "cave/crate/cage" condo, was a friendly, playful, nonaggressive Staffordshire terrier named Plato. He was a good dog. But he had suffered the misfortune of being born what he was, "this kind of a dog," and then harshly judged and pegged a mean type, a grave danger to society. This he was not! No way was he this! What he was, was a philosopher. He had become quite the thinker, this little one, locked up alone and having so much time on his paws.

Plato's thought: "This is a box, a crate. A stifling, confining, and torturous small thing. It is not a condo. A condominium is an apartment. A space, usually a comfortable space. A space that has rooms, with ceilings. Some of these ceilings are wonderfully high ones. It has bedrooms to sleep in, living rooms to entertain in and to watch a little TV in, or maybe to listen to some good music on a stereo. Dining rooms to eat in or to use as an office. Kitchens to cook in, and the all-purpose bathroom for everything else.

"A condo has windows for light and air, to see and breathe the world. A condo has doors that can be opened and closed by the tenant. That means freedom to enter and leave. To have company or not, depending on your mood. A condo has beautiful paintings on the walls, paintings that one can enjoy looking at.

"All I have on my walls, in this stifling crate, are shadows that change, move around, and disappear, and then come back the next day. Nothing in my crate is permanent except me. It's enough to break a body and a mind.

"A cage is not a condo either. A cage is a cage. A confining cell with bars. That's all it is. Anyone locked up in a cage knows he's locked up in a cage. They are not happy, secure individuals. They are not resting peacefully and happily in a condo, no matter who says they are.

"No one wants to be locked up or kept in a box, cage, or crate. Solitary confinement is what it is, and that's all it is, and nothing else. No matter how you pull it, twist it, cut it up, whenever you put it back together, it still comes up solitary confinement. It's used as a punishment for the worst criminals in a penal system. What did I do? What law did I break? Why should lies justify means? That's what I would like to know.

"I was told I would be in this solitary crate for two years. That that was how long it would take to teach me all the necessary social graces. Then and only then would I be trusted enough to live in the beautiful, spacious condominium outside this crate.

"Two years for a trust to be invested in my person, to be taught and imprinted, permanently, so that it could not ever be broken. That I would not behave in a wild, reckless, and irresponsible manner when I would finally be given my taste of freedom. It's been more than three years, and I'm still here, and I haven't tasted anything that tastes like freedom yet."

"Dogs need lots of exercise, to keep them healthy and fit. To calm them down, so they don't destroy the house. It wears them out so they will sleep all day and stay out of trouble."
—Many experts in USA, circa late twentieth century

Plato's thought: "When I'm taken out of this crate for a stroll and a pit stop, a strict procedure and protocol have to be followed. I have to be dressed properly. Why are a mask, choke, prong, and chain the proper raiments for me? And this I must wear before I am allowed to go out on the street to pee? To pee, perchance to breathe a little fresh air. Nobody likes to wear these archaic torture devices. They hurt. They hurt back in those days, and they still hurt now.

"The muzzle is placed over my head covering my face completely and preventing me from opening my mouth. That's one way to stop someone from getting their ideas out into the world. To shut a philosopher up. Maybe they're afraid of what I might say. Or maybe they're afraid I might yawn, showing all of my teeth in the process, and people might get the wrong idea.

"That's all I can figure out, that's all I can come up with at this time. I'm trying to understand the nature of what they are doing to me. What is the purpose of this weird behavior? What are the roots of this reality? Where is the point of fact?"

"He must wear a muzzle, he puts fear in the hearts of all. He might try to eat someone on his comings and goings from the 'crate, cage, condo' so he has to wear the mask. Others will be more comfortable around him. He should understand that. After all, these devils can be unpredictable. They can turn on you in an instant. They can attack without warning."
—Many experts in USA, circa late twentieth century

Plato's thought: "I don't like this mask, it's like wearing handcuffs on my face. I suddenly feel I can identify with Dumas's man in the iron mask, poor guy. He didn't do anything wrong either. But reality was remade in his case also."

Now with the muzzle mask securely buckled around Plato's head and face, so he couldn't bite anyone, next came the prong and choke collars. These apparatus were extremely important, so that he could be held back, to make him walk nicely and stop him from lunging at anyone. If he tried any funny stuff, he could be choked into submission and learn that he had better listen, or else.

And finally, a three-foot-long, two-inch-wide, quarter-inch-thick leather leash, to keep him short-leashed and under total control at all times, was hooked on to all the other "safety restraining devices," which some consider humane.

Where is the point of fact? Where is reality, when you need it? Where has it all gone?

> "The prong collar doesn't tear into the neck, the choke collar doesn't choke, the buckled muzzle doesn't bother him at all. As you can plainly see, he's comfortable and he can breathe quite easily. The short leash isn't really short, it's a reduced-length leash; as you can plainly see, he has freedom to walk. All in all he has as much freedom as anyone."
>
> —Many experts in USA, circa late twentieth century

Plato's thought: "I can't breathe, I can't walk, and I'm hanged at every step. I have trouble pissing and taking a dump. Every time I try to do one or the other, I'm either hanged, choked, or stepped on, because of the short leash and the other binding devices, considered humane, but which tie me up totally, body and soul. Voice of reason, where are you?

"I am thoroughly embarrassed by the reactions of people who see me dressed this way. They freeze or throw themselves out of my path, screaming and terrified; some even pass right out.

"With all this embarrassment on the outside, with all this intimidation and restraints that are put on me, with all this horrible torturing of my body, I would rather stay locked in a crate and be left alone. Because that's all the peace that's going to be allowed me."

> "You see, I told you so, he loves his crate, he goes right in it. I can't get him out of it at times. It's just like I said, dogs

are 'cave' animals. They love the security of living in a cave/
crate/cage/condo."
　　　　　　—Many experts in USA, circa late twentieth century

Plato's thought: "I don't feel secure living in this crate. I am a
social creature and I need to interact with the world. I don't need
to be here for security. Even if I lived in the wild and wanted to
be in a cave, I could still come and go as I please and bring all of
my family and invite all my friends to be with me, if I so choose.
It's a matter of choice, and to have freedom of choice is important to all. It's part of the constitution of any great republic.

"However, any prisoner that is kept in a small and controlled
confinement for long periods of time will get used to it. He will
feel secure in it, and he will grow to accept it, as if that's all
there is in life. Especially when that is all there is in his life."

Plato wanted to make a statement, he wanted to make a difference. He wanted to put things right. But to Plato's dismay,
there were so . . . many experts, USA, circa late twentieth century, and all were making so many grand pronouncements. It
was enough to get a believer in reality and reason real dizzy.

What was the answer? What could he do? How could he get
his message across and tell everyone that these crates, cages,
muzzles, chokes, and prongs really hurt? They are inhumane,
not humane contraptions. And the excuses that are made for
them are even worse. Those experts that say these things are
not detrimental to the dog's health and well-being should be
asked to wear them or to be put inside them. Then they might
have a view of reality as it really is and give us some true information and good feedback for a change.

Plato's thought: "O Zeus! Loose your powers! This helpless,
misunderstood, voiceless, dungeoned small citizen needs your
help! And needs it bad! I'm held captive in a world that doesn't
understand me, or my kind. Help me! Loose the powers of the

gods! Reality has been remade, and I am paying the price for its distortion!"

Plato looked up in the sky, as if he were praying. We couldn't be sure because he was so covered up by the mask and the choke and the prong. He could just have been trying to yawn. I guess we'll never know.

Did Zeus hear him? We don't know that either, but a strange phenomenon occurred. Lightning flashed, thunder cracked, and the spot where Plato's "modern caveman" once stood, grinning and holding that three-foot leather leash, at that very moment became a large rock. A rock that looked like a crate. A crate with three small openings that were wired crisscross. Inside, tightly packaged, was the figure of the former owner of the beautiful condominium.

All dogs, from that moment on, made it a point to visit the Rock and leave their marks on it.

The "late modern caveman" had an ex-wife, who finally collected on their divorce settlement. She took the beautiful condominium and everything in it, including Plato.

Her first moves were to get rid of all the "late modern caveman"'s personal belongings, and this included the crate/cage/cave/condo prison and all of the torturous restraining devices that had kept Plato shackled. The ex-wife, believing that Plato was responsible for all of her good fortune, repaid him royally, with a wonderful life of luxury and good fresh food, especially those sweet, sweet pastries from the Aegean.

Plato's final thought: "Life is sweet, indeed, and indubitably."

You, the Guardian of the Gate, the Keeper of the Keys

The third element of the triangle is you. You are the guardian of your canine or feline companion, the keeper of the keys.

Your ability to understand, to apply what you learn, and to distinguish between the real and the imaginary, the fact and the fiction—and let us tell you, there's plenty of fiction going around—will be absolutely crucial. Your job is to think, and do.

A rose is a rose is a rose. A rose by any other name is still a rose. Many call a choke collar a "release" collar. No matter what you call a choke collar, it still chokes first and foremost. That is what it was designed to do and that is what it does.

When a man is hanged, he's choked to death by the strangulation of the noose. This is called a hanging. When the hanged man is cut down, the choking pressure on the noose is "released," then the noose is removed. But you wouldn't call this a "release noose." And for sure you wouldn't blame the hangee for choking himself.

Anyone who tells you that you are not choking your dog by using a choke collar, or that the dog is choking himself because he is pulling, or that a "choke collar" is really a "release collar," should be chokingly released from the conversation. It's a "release" myth.

Those that tell you to use a choke collar are getting themselves off the choking hook by telling you it doesn't hurt the dog one bit. Some don't want to face that they are choking their dog by using a choke collar. They can get themselves off the hook, and not be responsible for the pain they're putting their dog through, by listening to the double-talk of the pseudo-quick-fixers, and to any rationale, even if it doesn't make sense, that might make it all right. If they have to block out reality and keep their heads up in the clouds or down in the sand, so be it. "I'm not choking him, he's doing it to himself."

A choke is a choke.

The same goes double/triple for the prong/pinch collar. In this case you're asked to disbelieve your own eyes as well as your ears. You'll hear the justification that this collar doesn't hurt the dog. It certainly does. It rips into the skin and it does put holes in the dog's neck. These holes you can see for yourself, providing the dog is not wearing a scarf to hide them.

Those who tell you this collar doesn't hurt and that there is no pain, and that the dog can take it, ask them to put this collar on themselves, give it a good pull or two, and then ask for a comment. If they're able to comment with their pronged sore throat, and a couple of holes in their neck.

Pain. It is said that a dog or a cat can take pain, more pain than we can. That they have a high tolerance for pain and a lower awareness of it. And that pain is tied in with intelligence. If the latter part of this theory holds true, we know many, many people who are living pain-free lives.

Dogs and cats have a nervous system, which means they can feel. And if they can feel, they can feel pain. They do have a brain; that means they're intelligent beings, and they do think. With thinking and feeling they can think about pain and feel pain. Their supersenses are better developed than ours in every way, which means, if anything, dogs and cats would have a lower tolerance to pain and probably feel pain more than you do.

The only difference here is that they have no way of communicating to you, in your language, that you are hurting them. You have to be more sensitive and aware of your animal, so that you won't miss the distress signals when they are being sent out to you.

Now, let's give you our pain test and see if you can take it. Put your hand in your dog's mouth. Step on his tail, and tell us how much pain he felt. You can measure this by the amount of teeth marks left on your hand and the depth that the teeth went in. If you run bleeding to the emergency room in a hospital, congratulations, you achieved a ten on the pain tolerance test, and you'll know, beyond any doubt, that your dog feels pain, and he also feels your pain. And he will, most likely, feel terrible for causing you pain in our pain test. Now you'll have some idea of your dog's pain threshold, and of yours.

Face restraints, such as muzzles, or ones that twist the head or ones that close the mouth, or any other creative face or head controller, will have side effects. Restraints on the face will rub the face raw when pulled, no matter how "gentle" you're told the restraint is. It might be gentle-looking to you, but look closer, and you'll see a whole 'nother story.

Since a dog uses his mouth in the way you use your hands, when you put a muzzle or any other kind of restraint on his head or face, it's like you going out into the world with your hands being locked behind your back in handcuffs. A helpless feeling, and not a nice feeling at all.

But the contraption that causes the most problems in a dog's life, the contraption that causes physical and psychological effects that will last the life of the dog, is the "wonderful" crate/cage/condo. This isolation box will have the most insidious and far-reaching effects of all the contraptions that man ever made to control his best friend, "the dog."

The wonderful reality-stretch here, the tunnel-vision answer drawn for locking the dog up in that thing, is that the dog is a "cave" animal and needs these caves for his privacy and security, and that's why he is given a crate/cage/condo, a home of his own and a place to think. If you stop to think a minute, this argument is totally ludicrous. It is just not true. Dogs are social creatures. They like family settings. They love to bond with families, with people, with you.

Even an animal living in the wild, one that might choose a cave to live in, can leave anytime he wants to; he is not locked up in the cave by himself and can bring home company anytime he so chooses. And if he doesn't enjoy his company, he can throw them out without worrying about any social consequences.

Or, he might, in a philanthropic gesture, give all these socializing buddies of his this now-crowded cave and get himself a new one. One with better views and higher ceilings and more rooms, including bathrooms. Or, he might decide he never liked the cave lifestyle after all and prefers sleeping out under the stars with a full moon. Will your dog have these options in his cage/crate/condo?

To keep your dog in a crate or a cage is to bond him to that. You will lose the wonderful social interaction that you wanted from your dog in the first place. The dog will develop a "crate mentality," a feeling of security in that crate/cage, a feeling of being totally secure, away from you, in that box.

If your dog is frightened, hurt, or in any danger, he will not look to you for security. His security will be transferred to a closet, under a bed, any hiding place, including his crate, if he can get into it.

He has no way of learning that you are his security blanket. How is he to know that you will help him if he is frightened or hurt, if he spends most of his time locked up? If you bring the dog up and bond him to you, then if there is any kind of problem, any real danger, or just lightning and thunder, the frightened animal won't run away from you and hide. He will run to you for help and guidance, for security and direction. If there is a fire in your house, he will run to you for safety and life and not run into his cage and die. If you know how to bring your dog or cat up right and how to give guidance and direction, then he will grow up trusting you for his security.

The justification given for this crate thing is that the dog is a "cave" animal, that he loves and needs his "cave." But the actual reasons for putting the dog in the crate/cage are not so altruistic; they are merely to stop him from soiling or destroying your home, or he is locked up when you want him out of the way.

As for those who insist on calling this crate/cage a condo, it would prove instructive for them to live in these "condos" for a length of time and let us know what it feels like to live in this luxurious form of condominium living.

Schools of Thought, Analogies, Gossip, and Chitchat

There are behavioral analogies deduced from the social upbringing and lives of animals living in the wild and their social interaction with each other. Then training techniques are formulated around these deductions made from the behavioral analogies. These techniques are then used as the foundation and structure to "train" your dog and cat, who are domestic animals, have never been in the wild, who for generations haven't lived in the wild, weren't born in the wild, and don't even know what wild is.

Dogs and cats live at home with you. What is wild about that? They are distant cousins of their wild counterparts. Just as you have a wild past and some distant cousins.

How our ancestors lived in the wild has little practical application for us and the way we live today. When was the last time you went in quest of fire? And we don't mean turning on the microwave or the stove.

However bizarre, strange, impractical, or impossible these straight-into-your-home-from-the-wild techniques are, this has not prevented whole schools of thought, misguided theories, gossip, chitchat, and silly analogies from appearing and defining ways to control, live with, and "train" dogs and cats.

A wild dog, a lion, or a wolf will pin another of his own species down and hold him down with his mouth around the throat to show dominance. Or they will hunt, pin, kill, and eat another species for dinner. It's successful, it works, and it has worked for these species since the dawn of time.

This will not work for you. You're not a lion, a wild dog, a wolf, or a saber-toothed tiger, for that matter. You are man or woman, as the case may be. You have a small mouth not meant for holding or eating prey, unless the prey has been fried, sautéed, grilled, or poached, and then put on a plate, with a pretty design, and served to you to be eaten with a knife and a fork, fancy or plain, silver or plastic.

Man or woman may have a bigger mouth than the others for expressing themselves verbally, for eating in restaurants and yelling about the service, but it's still a useless mouth for grabbing, pinning, or killing live prey. This is impractical for you to do and could be dangerous as well. Unless you could turn yourself into a werewolf; then you might have a better success with your mouth.

Bandied about and in vogue at the moment are two techniques on how you should stop your dog, if he is aggressive, from chasing after and attacking another dog. These two bizarre and impractical methods have been brought to you straight out of the wild and thrown down right on your doorstep.

If your dog decides to take off after another dog, you are told to chase after him and get him before a fight ensues. Get him in flight, if you can, catch him and grab him, if you can, snatch him up, if you can, and then throw him down and roll him over onto his back, if you can, and then pin him down, if you can, and hold his mouth shut at the same time, if you can, and tell him, "No!" "Bad," "Sit," "Cut," if you can.

Maybe if you have a large net, a few fast friends, a gun with a tranquilizing dart that works in seconds, or if you are as swift as a cheetah or as fast as a gazelle, you might stand a chance. If not, you don't.

Or, you might try the other technique to curb your aggressive dog. Get down at eye level with your big, bad bully. Stare him down with a hot, penetrating gaze, ferociously growl at him, and keep it up, the staring and the growling, until your big, bad bully backs down, turns his head, and walks away, browbeaten and thoroughly broken by your nonviolent and humane technique. You might even offer him a cookie for staring him into submission, showing him you really care for him.

With the mouth that you've got, you can certainly do a lot of growling all right. And with the ability to make faces, faces that no other animal can duplicate, you can do a lot of face-making for sure. You've got those two talents going for you, but the rest of your solution is a pretty lame game. Truth to tell, the growling and staring aren't such a big deal. If anything, your dog might look at you funny, and then again he might bite your nose, but you're not going to stop him from being aggressive this way. You'll lose. And after you've lost, you can then go to the muzzle, the choke, the prong, the electrical devices, or the chain on a pulley in the backyard. And if these fail, you can give your wild thing away, with a wild excuse.

Flight-Flipping Ferocious Freddy

A call from California; she is an investment banker. "My dog, Freddy," she says, "is the most aggressive dog I've ever seen when I take her outside. She was adopted. I think she was abused. That's what they told me at the shelter. She attacks other dogs. I think it's because she was abused by other dogs, so it is not really her fault. I understand how she feels, but I still have to stop it.

"I've done all the proper 'training' things. I got on eye level with her and growled; that didn't work. I tried grabbing her and flipping her when she got aggressive with other dogs. This was impossible. She is sixty-plus pounds. How am I to grab a dog in flight and flip her over? She is not a stationary pancake that you can easily flip over. Is this flight-flipping necessary to stop her aggression?

"First, I couldn't catch her, to attempt the flight flip, so I put a leash on her. The next time when she tried to run after other dogs, I was able to reel in the leash. I grabbed her and tried to flip her. Didn't work. I couldn't knock her down and roll her over. Instead, I fell down and she wound up dragging and pulling me about a hundred feet. She totaled me. My clothes were torn up, my elbows and knees were skinned, and I got all ripped up and filthy.

"Those techniques sounded all right; as a 'trainer' explained to me, in the wild, animals run after prey, grab the prey, knock the prey down, flip the prey over, pin them, and eat them. If they want. Or, they just might be telling another of their own kind 'to behave' themselves and who's 'in charge around here.'"

Don't use eye-level eyeballing or flight-flipping for aggressive dogs. You're only a primate, a slow-moving one at that. Learn how to capitalize on the abilities that you do have and that can put you on top of any situation.

But this information had come down to the banker from an expert. Maybe a flight-flipping, eyeballing dog expert.

We told this California investment banker to invest in learning about our Magic Touch. No flipping, no flopping, no flying down the streets, the roads, the beaches, no "catch as catch can," no scraping of your knees and elbows, and no tearing of your clothes. Just a plain, simple hand toss, letting your Magic Touch do the walking and the talking.

Most of the techniques that animals use to establish themselves socially, to control or to educate each other, work successfully for them, but will not work for you. You are not experienced in their worldly ways, their customs, their mores, and their belief systems.

The social behavior and interactions of animals that live with you have a different set of rules and priorities. Ours is a completely different world and needs a completely different way of teaching. You don't want wild animals to be your professors and guides. It's your responsibility to think things through. If it doesn't make sense to you, it probably doesn't make sense at all.

Out of the Blue: Grandma's Lore

The little boy was running out the door; he was late for school. His sharp-eyed grandma spotted the ripped sleeve and the missing button on his shirt. "A new shirt your momma bought you? And this is what you do to it? Get in here, I'll fix it," she said. "I can't, Grandma, I'm late for school," the little boy said as he tried desperately, but in vain, to get away from his grandma and out the door.

Grandma, with the speed of a winged Achilles, flew across the kitchen and grabbed him by his cheek. She pulled him back inside, sat him down at the kitchen table, put her hand to her chest, and now giving him some real guilt, with her passive-aggressive nature, she told him how he had almost given her heart failure and conniptions!

The eight-year-old boy was in a panic. "I'm sorry, Grandmother. I didn't mean to almost give you heart failure, I just gotta get to school—I'm late." Grandma, now seeing that she was in full control of the situation, that her grandson wasn't moving for fear that he might cause other major health problems—and he loved his grandma, so he wouldn't want to ever do that—calmly spun around and got her all-purpose sewing kit.

Confidently, she threaded the needle in one shot, while he anxiously watched her, looking for any critical signs of another attack of some sort. Then she took a piece of pumpernickel from the bread box, stuffed the piece in his mouth, and told him to chew. The little boy wanted to tell Grandma that he wasn't hungry and that he had eaten breakfast earlier, but he couldn't talk because of the giant piece of pumpernickel she had stuffed in his mouth.

Then, with great skill, Grandma sewed the ripped sleeve and put on the button. When it was all over, and everything was fixed, the little boy got up, the pumpernickel bread already swallowed, and asked his Grandma, "Why did you put the bread in my mouth and make me eat it?" "Don't question your grandma," she said. "But let me tell you, since you wouldn't take your shirt off and since you were in such a big hurry, I had no choice but to put the bread in your mouth, so that I wouldn't, if I ever made a mistake, but mind you I don't make mistakes, but the little chance that I did make the mistake, and stick you with the needle, I wouldn't sew your brains together. And don't think this is a joke; my mother taught me this in the old country. If you're wearing something and it gets sewn, while it's on you, it could very well happen that your brains could be sewn together, and you need those nice little brains so when you grow up you can become a doctor or a lawyer or even the president of the United States. Now get to school and don't be late." He was late anyway. Grandma's lecture took too long.

Grandma also believed that eating was a good cure for anything and everything, for anger, depression, frustration, and worrying, and for luck—eating would solve all your problems.

121

Knocking on wood, crossing your fingers, and a little salt-tossing over the shoulder also worked wonders.

We love our grandmas and much of their folklore, traditions, and old-country superstitions. Our grandmas got us through hard times and got us to school without ripped clothes, and they always kept us well fed and happy most of the time. They stepped in to help us when our parents got angry with us.

The flip side of superstition, gossip, and hearsay, however, can be harmful, especially when it comes to our dogs and cats. Strange ideas start out of the blue, from a casual conversation and chitchat, and then grow with a life of their own. On the subject of dogs and cats, everybody has something to say, whether it makes sense or not.

Small dogs bark more than large dogs. Dalmatians are unstable dogs. Afghans are stupid dogs. Terriers are difficult dogs to work with. Basset hounds are impossible dogs to stop from chewing things. Dachshunds are burrowing dogs and hide under blankets and quilts and can suffocate. Some dogs are good with children and some dogs are not. Some dogs should live in the country, other dogs should live in the city. Staffordshire terriers are vicious. German shepherds and rottweilers are unpredictable and dangerous.

As for cats, plenty of superstitions are going around. If a cat falls out of a window or from a tree, he will land on his feet. Long-haired cats are more affectionate than short-haired cats. Persian cats keep to themselves. Siamese cats are more social than other cats. Abyssinians are hard to live with. Black cats are bad luck, especially when they cross your path. But cats are also good luck. That cats can't be taught anything. That cats like to be alone, they are solitary creatures.

If you talk to a thousand people, the stories and the rumors about the dogs and cats on the list we gave will change. The good ones will become the bad ones, the dumb ones will become the intelligent ones, the difficult ones will become the easy ones. Around and around and around the stories go.

There is only one thing for sure: the misconceptions will go on and on and never stop. But the gossip can become more refined and more sophisticated, depending on who's doing the talking and who is doing the listening.

There was the Burnese mountain dog whose owner felt the Burnese dog needed mountains to climb. He resigned himself to trekking hours a day, searching for the highest mountain peaks in Central Park, so that his mountain dog would feel at home. Although this person never found a peak, the dog was happy with the small hills in Central Park. However, her real happiness was at home, sleeping in his bed and eating good food. Who cares about the mountain peaks?

Corky had a cat, a carnivorous animal, he was a flesh eater. Why was this carnivore, this flesh eater, why was this cat eating her potatoes with butter and sour cream, her creamed spinach, her asparagus lightly sautéed with herbs and extravirgin olive oil? And why did her carnivorous feline also want his very own piece of apple pie and ice cream? Was something wrong with this carnivorous cat? Or could this cat have some human ancestry? She had always thought that only people eat these things.

Maybe her cat was unusual? Maybe this cat wasn't really a cat? Maybe this cat was the reincarnation of a pharaoh, maybe even a Ramses or a King Tut? Her cat was an Egyptian cat, so why not? He certainly had the attitude. Her King Tut turned out to be most happy eating a balanced meal with her that included selections from the complete pyramid group of foods.

The only thing for certain about a specific breed of dog or cat is what the dog or cat looks like, the genetic imprint, and what sex. Everything else the cat or dog learns from day one is a *behavioral imprint*, one that is taught.

Dogs and cats all have the same supersenses. There are variations of these supersenses in the different breeds of dogs and cats. Some see better, some hear better, and some have a better sense of smell. Some are larger and some are smaller. Some are faster, some are slower. And they all run the color spectrum. That's it. There are no behavioral inferences to be drawn before they are born.

Linda from Detroit wanted to know, would her dog's nose turn pink if her dog drank out of a pink bowl? She said she had read this eye-opening information in an article. Could this be true? Yes, it definitely could. If the bowl had been recently painted pink and the paint hadn't yet dried, her dog could get a pink nose. If the dog stepped in the bowl, she could also get pink feet. If Linda took the bowl away from the dog, she could very well wind up with pink fingers.

When you hear someone talking about dogs and cats and not making sense, and going on and on in this not-making-sense vein, remember Grandma's solution. Put a large piece of bread in his mouth. It works wonders.

The Little Gladiators

As the gladiators were led into the coliseum, the crowds cheered, they roared and thumbed-up their favorites. The others, they jeered and thumbed-down or ignored completely, the ones they couldn't care less about.

These gladiators, some came bearing flags and sporting the colors of their house. Some wore armor and helmets; some wore nothing at all.

None of them had any real reason to fight. Except for the pure entertainment value of the show, or to save their necks.

Some of these warriors loved the games. But many others didn't want to be there, they wanted to be home in bed, or digging into a good, hot bowl of oatmeal and honey. But no, such was not to be, for these reluctant and always-hungry-for-a-good-meal gladiators.

Their sponsors, the ones who had dragged them here to the theater of battle, by leathers and chains, by thongs and ropes, didn't seem to care about the feelings of these protesting four-footed gladiators. If they had cared, they wouldn't have subjected them to this contest. They would not have fed them to the lions in the arena.

The gladiators were pushed on into the ring of fire, this fenced-in circle, in front of a gathered, excited crowd. This event would test their mettle, they could strut their stuff, show what they were made of, their value would be determined in the contests to come.

Even if the gladiators were bashful, even if they didn't want to go, even if they dug in their heels and refused to move, even if they tried to run away and hide, even if they tried to go home, tried to jump up into the arms of their sponsors, crying, pleading, and barking to be picked up and taken safely away, they weren't.

Their pleas were ignored and the misunderstood, reluctant players were pushed away by their sponsors. They were sent out to meet their fate. With an "it's good for you, you will love it, you will be with your own kind and socialize with them" attitude. Let the games begin!

The participants of dog-run society went swirling into action. A pastiche of form, color, and movement, of blurred figures running around and around and going nowhere. The steady, dizzying spin of a carousel of dogs in motion. But a wheel now spinning out of control.

Little do these sponsors know that the wild games of the dog run will not end at the gate's exit. You paid your price, now get your ride. You wanted a gladiator, now you've got one.

Popcorn, aka Attila

"Oh, my goodness! She never did that before, she's never bitten anybody. Never attacked another dog in her life. She's such a sweet little thing, wouldn't hurt a fly, this cute dog. Who'd know her better than me? I had this little girl since she was a puppy."

This person might have had her "sweet little thing" since the "sweet little thing" was a puppy, but she's not a puppy anymore, and she's no longer a "sweet little thing" either. This person unwittingly encouraged her dog to become an aggressive, biting one. The puppy didn't start out this way, nor was she born this way.

She had been born a white standard poodle, a puppy with a shiny black nose and distinctive gray-green eyes; they were odd for this breed. Once you saw her, you could never forget her.

It had been love at first sight. The puppy's quiet, shy, and vulnerable personality had been the clincher. That irresistible look on the puppy's face, the one saying, "Please, pick me up, hold me, and take me home," hadn't hurt either.

The "sweet little thing" had felt so soft and cuddly, and the bottoms of her feet had had the wonderful smell of popcorn. And so Popcorn became her nom de plume. But a new name, a more notorious one, one that had more the nasty smell of burning popcorn, was drifting her way: Attila.

How did this little popcorn puppy turn into such a terror? Attila. A rampaging fury of the dog runs, striking without warning and without mercy. She was an unleashed terror, bullying all who got in her way, and those that she thought might try, got it, too.

Her eyes brushed expertly across the assembled offerings of the day. White, sculpted brows, freshly trimmed by the groomer's hand, shaded the gray-green orbs of this intense, seasoned ruffian. She took a deep breath; the air was full of dog, it would be a good day for a fight.

She surveyed with unerring accuracy, a sweep of the gathered. Using her supersenses, she instinctively wandered through the bodies, the sounds, and the smells. She wondered as she wandered, "Who's next?" Her nose and her eyes picked up any physical weaknesses or ones of character. No failings would pass undetected. Neither time nor distance were obstacles. Not for this scanner.

That one, a shelter dog, was young and afraid, no need to waste energy there. A look would do the trick. This one was jet-lagged, he'd just flown in from Wyoming. He'd been drugged, boxed, and cargoed. No contest here. Wobbling and staggering from the drugs, he could hardly stand, let alone put up any resistance. Another time for him. Graybeard, that old one in the corner, he was easy. She ignored the rest. They had already been beaten into submission; they were no fun. Too easily controlled and converted, these would not add to her fame. Her blood was hot, she wanted action. Which way was glory? Where was it to be found? Who would be next to pay allegiance to Attila of the run? Which reluctant warrior of the gladiatorial group?

As she surveyed, a frisson of fear went through the assembly. Some cowered and rolled over, some moved aside quickly, out of her path, but they all knew they were not the one.

All at once, her gray-greens fixed on a target. Now she knew. She wanted the minstrel boy. The teller of the tall tales, the rhymer of rhymes, he of the crooked tail. He talked too much, had a big mouth; it was time to shut it. His recitations, his singsong verses, got on her nerves. Abelardo, the troubadour, would soon be singing castrato, when Attila got through with his music lesson. She would fix him, she would alter him, but good.

"The minute my vet gave me permission to take my puppy outside, I had her socializing with lots of other dogs for her emotional and physical development. I was told it was important for her to be around her own kind. She is so happy socializing in dog runs, and meeting other dogs on the street. It makes me feel good to see her happy. I also enjoy having these social moments with other people and their dogs. I find them refreshing. I learn so much about animal behavior and get so many 'training' tips in conversations.

"I would let her run free and go play in the dog runs. At first she was shy, and I had to push her into it. I had to tell her that being with these other dogs was good for her character and that she could learn so much from these other dogs.

"They would playfully chase her and knock her down. She would try to make her way back to me and run to hide between my legs. The other dogs would stop her. Even if she did get to me, I would shoo her away with a good push and encourage her to go, have fun, and enjoy herself with her friends. It worked. As time went by, she became sure of herself, very sociable, and played more with the other dogs.

"I was so proud of my little girl when I saw that she was starting to hold her own in the run. Then I was just bubbling with pride when she started to control the social activity of the groups in the run. She clawed, mouthed, and pulled as she made her way up the social ladder, until she became the dog in charge.

"She could now even tell the aggressive dogs to behave themselves, sometimes by mounting them playfully and sometimes by nipping at them playfully. She was so cute; there she was, my little girl in charge of everything, running the place.

"Then one day, for no reason at all, she went over to a dog. A newcomer, a boy dog with a broken tail. It looked funny, you know, crooked? She only wanted to playfully mount the other dog, in a friendly way. As they all do. I don't know why, but the other dog got nasty, turned around, and growled at Popcorn for no reason at all.

"Popcorn attacked this dog and bit him viciously, pinning him down by the throat. We all screamed 'Sit' and 'No,' but it didn't work. It took only a couple of minutes for the fight to be over. They had to take the bitten dog out of the run immediately and get him to an emergency clinic.

"I couldn't believe it. Popcorn had never hurt a dog in her life. Sure she might have 'nipped' other dogs or mounted them, but it was all in good spirits, and in fun. The other dog must have provoked her. He was a noisy dog, and he had a crooked tail, he just wasn't a dog-run-type dog. I hope they never bring that mean, aggressive dog back to our dog run. He ruined everything."

We hear this dog-run-socializing commentary frequently. And the outcomes are of little surprise. At the beginning, this Popcorn had been a sensitive puppy who didn't want to play with the other dogs. She was apprehensive of the other dogs, especially at such an early age, a vulnerable age. She wanted to be with the one person she thought she knew, the one person she felt she could trust with her life and well-being.

This person should have read the signs of a frightened puppy and been sensitive to her puppy's pleas for help. She could have picked her up and taken her out of the run at any time and prevented an incident that was just waiting to happen. She could have prevented her dog from turning into a biter.

When this person chased her puppy away from her and back to the other dogs, when she ignored all the distress signals and dismissed them as just playing, this puppy, who had come to her for help, now felt that she had nowhere to go for help. She had good reason to feel this way.

This is not a nice feeling for a puppy. Not a nice feeling for an adult dog. Having problems dealing with this kind of stress and fear is not nice for anyone to have to go through.

From now on Popcorn would have to take care of and be responsible for herself, for her own safety and well-being. It was grow-up-fast time now. Relying only on yourself is quite a task and a burden for a four-and-a-half-month-old puppy dog to handle all alone.

Handle it she did. She would lie down, roll on her back, cower, and let the other dogs mount her, bite her, and intimidate her in every way. All in the name of fun, games, and socializing.

Popcorn had only two options. Fight back or be knocked around forever. Nobody likes to be beaten up and intimidated. Nobody likes to be cornered like a rat. Not even a rat, not even a nice one.

Little by little, this nonaggressive, sensitive puppy started fighting back. Pulling herself up in the order of things. And Popcorn's owner, busily engrossed with the other dog people, discussing dog stuff and other social matters, failed to see that her popcorn dog was becoming an aggressive, biting dog.

Popcorn first started biting out of fear and self-defense. It worked. The other dogs left her alone. Then Popcorn saw the advantages and successes she could gain from this biting back. She could control things. Dogs would listen to her. Some rolled on their backs. She liked this.

She tested her techniques further. She attacked and bit nonaggressive younger dogs. As she gained confidence, she moved up to older and larger dogs, friendly, docile ones, ones who wouldn't fight back. As she continued to build her confidence, and because her actions went unchecked, unsupervised, she became a full-blown, nasty little bully.

She took on her competitors one by one, tearing them up, until she became the top dog in her dog run. And so it would go, the rule of Attila, until she herself would be toppled by a stronger, nastier, and more determined challenger.

All under the nose of the unaware dog owner, enthralled by the playful social interaction of dog-run society.

The torn-up dog that was hospitalized had been a nice, friendly dog who didn't want to be mounted or played around with. He had given out a signal, a leave-me-alone warning growl. Popcorn, now Attila, had felt that this dog should be dealt with, dispatched as fast and as viciously as possible, for talking back, so that there would be no return engagement. Let the other dogs of the run see what she, Attila, was capable of. Even if the other dog wasn't aggressive toward her, it no longer mattered.

This is a classic scenario. This happens in every part of the animal world where there is any competition. Dog runs could be safer if people could control their dogs. But it only takes that one person with that one uncontrolled dog to cause an injury to your dog.

Many dogs enjoy dog runs. And many dog owners enjoy watching their dogs run and play. Keep in mind that dogs, like people, don't all enjoy the same things. Be sensitive to your dog. Be aware of aggression. All dogs in a dog run must be under some kind of supervision and control.

People seem to be surprised when their nice dog suddenly becomes a biting, aggressive one. Or, they are surprised when they suddenly have a dog that is frightened and insecure. These character changes don't happen overnight. They develop slowly. By misreading the signals, you could end up with a new dog on your hands, a different dog from the one you started out with, one that you might not like, an Attila when all you wanted was a Popcorn. These problems are completely avoidable.

On the Street

Conflict doesn't only happen in dog runs, where dogs are turned loose and allowed to run free. It can happen just as easily when you are out walking your dog on a leash. Confrontations happen every day on the street, and in any public place. There's a chance for a combative altercation as long as there are dogs that love to bully other dogs, or dogs who have been attacked and bullied themselves, and as long as there are dog owners who will not face the fact that their dogs are not toys to be wound up and trotted out for show-and-tell.

Dogs do not see the dog walk the same way their owners do. It's a serious matter to them when dog meets dog. Puppies trust the world; they are young and innocent and want to play with everyone they see. Some adult dogs act the same way.

But once an aggressive dog attacks, bites, or intimidates that nice little dog that is rolled over on his back being submissive, then that nice little dog will think all other dogs can and will act that way. So the nice little dog, in turn, becomes first defensive, then aggressive, and finally out of control altogether. Or, that little dog can become a frightened and shy one. This is just plain common sense.

Unless you can control your dog and know what to do if other dogs try to annoy, intimidate, or attack him, your dog will not trust you at all. You won't be worth a hill of beans to him. As far as your dog is concerned, you will have failed as a parent figure. Then, don't be surprised if your dog becomes frightened of everything, won't listen to you, and won't walk with you.

Your dog could very well become a biting dog. He might even take a bite out of you if you get on his nerves.

Practice some street manners and a little social decorum. Manners go a long way in preventing any altercations. When two dogs meet on the street, it doesn't mean the dogs should jump all over each other, mount each other, smell each other, get down and roll in the dirt with each other, and just in general knock each other around. Don't force dogs to be together and socialize. Don't shove them into each other.

Should someone ignore you when you ask them to "please leave my dog alone," you will have to find other ways to get them to respect you, your dog, and your wishes. Sometimes it won't be nice. If you are given a remark or a dirty look, well, it's not the worst thing that can happen to you in this life.

Dogs can hurt one another in a fight, there are no winners, and it is frightening to be part of a dogfight. Breaking one up is a dangerous proposition. Not only for the parties directly involved, but also for anyone close by, who had the bad luck that day to be in the wrong place at the wrong time.

Ask permission to touch another person's dog, especially those with a new puppy. When others have a dog, it doesn't mean you can automatically go right up and grab the dog, play with him, pounce on him, fawn all over him, feed him, or do anything you feel like with him. He is their dog. He belongs to them. Not to you. Ask first, it's polite. And do take no as an answer. You wouldn't behave this way with someone's child. Parents will usually not let a stranger talk to or put their hands on their child. Why shouldn't it be the same way with you and your dog?

Family groups or units, human or animal, stay together and play together. When you bring a dog or a cat into your home, he is brought up as part of your family. If you bring an outsider into your home, you shouldn't take for granted that all will get along and be friends. They could become combatants, they could wildly get to know each other, or they could mark off territories in your house, and not with pencil and paper. They will mark it off their own way, with yellow ink.

There are billions of human beings in this world; that doesn't mean that they can walk into your house and take your television set, or whatever they want, using the excuse that "we're all human beings, after all, just one big happy family."

With packs of wolves, hyenas, lions, wild dogs, and human animals, even though particular groups are of the same species that doesn't guarantee automatic acceptance. If one of these wolf packs, lion prides, or human families encroaches onto another's territory, they are not warmly greeted. This is called trespassing. And intruders anywhere are dealt with harshly. You can't always expect a square dance, a social function, or a civilized debate. There's not always a community house for the interchange of ideas. No. Intruders can be chased, attacked, and even killed.

Puppies shouldn't be allowed to socialize with other dogs, or people, unless and until they are bonded to you, 100 percent. You will know when this bonding is solid: when your puppy leaves other animals and people alone, no matter what the enticements may be—food bribes, massage bribes, or such. When your puppy comes to you and stays by you, until you give him permission to play. And when you say playtime is over, there is no argument. Making this connection with your puppy shouldn't take more than a few weeks. Don't let the popcorn burn.

We always say there are only two things your dog will get from another dog: bad habits and parasites. Socializing with other dogs will not teach your dog any social graces or anything constructive. If you are going to indulge in dog socializing, make sure you are in full control of all the social functions.

And if you want to have many animals of the same or different species in your home, the same principle goes. Make sure that they all know that you can take care of things and protect each and every one of them, from either outside dangers and problems or from each other.

Dogs with Spirit

Where do you draw the lines of control and spirit; where do they meet? How do you separate them? Some are concerned that to stop a dog's wild playing with other dogs or people, to curb their dog's "spirit" in any way, shape, or form, might have some deleterious consequences and hinder their dog's emotional growth.

Because of these concerns, their dogs are allowed to grow up uncontrollably wild and do as they please. Behave like bulls in a china shop if they want to. Destroy your home, if they want to. Jump all over anyone at any time, and anywhere, if they want to. Then, all of the bad actions of these spoiled brats, these "spirited poltergeists," are brushed aside and labeled "spirit." It is the "spirit" explanation and excuse. You know, "boys will be boys," "dogs will be dogs," "cats will be cats," and "spirits, good or bad, wanted or unwanted, will be spirits." Get a ghost buster for the "spirited" dog, maybe he can help you tame your wild "spirit."

An awful lot of the most "spirited" dogs and cats are living in animal shelters, a halfway-house solution between this world and the next one. When no one could tolerate or put up with their uncontrollable "spirit" any longer, they join the other "spirits" in that other "spirited" world. We are talking dead dogs and cats here. A situation that never had to happen in the first place.

The other sad side of the "spirit" excuse is that the people who had these dogs and cats didn't believe that these dogs and cats were smart enough to know any better, that they had been somehow coded this way, to be wild, or that they were just not smart enough to be taught anything.

When you're bringing up your children, you teach them, or at least you try to teach them, how to grow up and behave properly. You take on this responsibility and give it the seriousness it deserves. Your dog is not a toy for the world to play with, he's your responsibility, so control his "spirit," teach him some manners and a little social decorum as well.

The Tiny New World Explorer . . . Bringing Up Baby

Many breeders and experts, including many veterinarians, believe that a puppy should stay with his mother until he is approximately seven or eight weeks old. Some experts believe that puppies should stay with their mother for even longer than that.

Their reasoning is that the puppy should be socialized with others in the litter, so the pup will learn about and feel secure around other dogs. In addition, the puppy's mother is expected to teach her offspring all about our world, how to avoid and maneuver around the everyday dangers in a human society, and how to be fully prepared for its demands, so that these little ones can successfully thrive in their new homes with us. A major school of thought has grown up around this philosophy.

No matter how you try to make it so, and no matter how you try to make it fit, this school of thought doesn't make much sense at all.

A puppy, after bonding with his birth mother and socializing with his brothers and sisters, still enters the outside world all alone. A tiny explorer, he will be setting off on his voyage of discovery with only his identification documents, a small parcel of food, and possibly a piece of luggage, a box.

We recommend when your new-world, small explorer arrives with his small parcel of food, if it is dry, throw it away. And give him something good, a hot meal after his voyage—maybe Italian cuisine for Columbus, meatballs and spaghetti with a side of sautéed escarole, will do him just fine and he will feel warm and welcomed from day one. You can also get rid of the box.

But the chances are that your little explorer is not bringing his mother and all the rest of his biological family with him into his new home, your house. Unless, in a weak moment, you bought the whole family.

Everything the puppy encounters will be completely different, brand-new, and surprising. A total change from what he was familiar with in the protected environment of his mother and the rest of the gang.

You are going to be his everything. The puppy arrives with an empty slate. You will be taking on the roles of his new mother, his father, his brother or sister, and definitely you will be his teacher. He will be learning everything about anything from you.

How would the puppy, by staying with his mother for seven, eight weeks or longer, learn anything about his new life to be? How will she teach him about cars, traffic, other animals, poisons, other people, bicycles, skaters on Rollerblades, electrical appliances, swimming pools, or the beach? How will bonding to his birth mother help the new puppy?

There is nothing about this bonding-with-the-mother theory that will help the young puppy and that will benefit him with you. Even girl puppies, who will learn how to take care of their own young from their mother, will have been taught this parenting skill within the first four weeks of life.

An exception would be puppies who are being bred for a

specific purpose, one where a dog-pack mentality is necessary, for example, working dogs on a farm or ranch. These puppies will definitely be living, socializing, and working with other dogs, in pairs or larger groups. But even here, in these environments, although the puppy will stay and work with other dogs as a team, he still has to learn to take direction from a human.

This herding and grouping mentality is of no use to you, especially if you live in a one-bedroom apartment where the other party living with you is a parakeet. In that case you want to teach your dog not to herd the bird, but to leave the bird be.

By the by, dogs who are "herders" are not born that way; this "herding" instinct is not in their blood, they must be taught this skill. So if your dog is "herding" you and yours, by biting your ankles or anyone else's, stop him, because he is not "herding" from some genetic, ancient instinct that has to be respected and honored and accepted. What he is doing is being a major pain in the ass and "hurting" you and yours. Throw something at the hurting "herder" and reverse thousands of years of genetic herding instinct in a toss.

It is to your great advantage and in the puppy's best interest to get him away from his litter and to bring him home with you as early as possible. This should happen when the puppy is weaned. Weaning generally takes place at about five weeks, and sometimes sooner.

At this point, the young puppy can develop a strong relationship with you. If you do your homework and learn how to bring your puppy up right, then everything the puppy sees, hears, or smells can be directed in a way so that you will really enjoy having this little guy around. The puppy now learns from his new mother, you, whatever your gender might be.

To us, this is socializing the right way—keeping your new puppy with you, bonding him to you, forging the strong bonds that will last a lifetime, teaching him about you, and your life.

Set up all the positive habits from day one. Teach him from day one. He learns immediately, from day one. Don't wait until your puppy is six months old to teach him his p's and q's, as many advise. If you do, then you are going to have to break six months of self-learned p's and q's, and few of them will be ones that you would want to live with.

And if you lock up your tiny explorer in the brig during these early puppy formative years, you are breaking a promise — an implied contract, a trust, a commitment that you made when you brought this little fella into your home to share your life and to be your buddy. Don't break the faith, keep it.

The Wandering One

Your puppy explorer must be supervised. He has an insatiable curiosity, many creative ideas, and he's just busting out with all his youthful energy to discover and explore this new world of his, this new territory, your home.

But this exploring, inquisitive pathfinder must be shown the proper maps and coordinates and the right paths so that he doesn't stray off these paths and into your closet. There he may very well find, to your dismay, a couple of shoes or suits he's never seen before and he might want to check them out, to know more about them, what they smell like, what they taste like, what they look like close up — real close up.

After he is thoroughly satisfied with his discoveries, the explorer will leave a flag so that you, and anyone else who goes into that closet, will know that he, the little explorer, discovered it.

You might not want to find his flags in your closet on your shoes and suits. Having discovered closets, he will now move on to other new worlds, the bedroom, the living room, and the rest of your home. You could find the explorer's flags everywhere. Your house could look as if it's been surveyed for a construction site, and sometimes at night, when you get up for a necessary stroll, you might discover a flag on the bottom of your foot. So, it will be necessary to manage your small explorer, range in your wandering rover.

The Explorer's Governor—the Tether

The governor of your intrepid explorer will be the tether. The tether will allow the explorer to see and visualize his territories, who's coming and going, what's going on around him. He can listen to any sounds, the usual ones or new ones, even watch television. In the kitchen, he can see and smell what's for breakfast, lunch, and dinner. In the den, he can help you work on the computer. In the bedroom, he can nap with you during the day and sleep with you at night. When you shower in the morning, he can be with you if you like company there. All of this without one accidental, unwanted flag left anywhere.

Also, your little explorer will never, ever have a low, crated ceiling over his head or be closed in by crate or cage bars or walls to limit him in any way, physically or psychologically. He'll feel good knowing that he can take a real good stretch at any time he wants to, and he can do it in any direction he chooses.

The tether will also fit in your pocket, enabling you to bring your young explorer to other home environments, and he will love to go with you on these outings. The tether will govern his every move, and you won't lose him in uncharted territory. Therefore, your small visitor will be welcome wherever he goes and your hosts won't have to worry about their territories being reclaimed with the distinctive discovery flags of your explorer.

You'll find it easier to carry the lightweight tether in your pocket than to have to lug a heavy, cumbersome crate or cage around on your back, as you go from room to room. If you have a vacation home, it's easier to put a tether in your pocket when you travel than to put a crate or a cage into your car and lug it from state to state, and then pull it, carry it, or push it around from room to room in your vacation home when you get there for a "vacation."

The governing tether will also teach your explorer how to accept a collar, plain or fancy, and a leash to match, all while you sleep, work, cook, read, or do nothing at all.

How to Construct the Tether

Your dog will be able to chew right through a leather or nylon tether no matter how thick it is. As long as he can get his teeth around it, it will go. You'll need something he cannot chew through; you'll need a chain, a 2.5-millimeter, welded curb chain.

It's the same chain used to make a chain leash, or a chain choke collar. It should be eighteen inches long, but no longer than that. Years of experience, and trial and error, proved that with more than eighteen inches you're risking a strong possibility that your dog will find toilet-going room and use it, indiscreetly. Less than eighteen inches won't give him enough comfortable sitting, lying down, or stretching-out room. Eighteen inches is perfect.

You'll also need two S-hooks—these are self-explanatory, they look exactly like the letter S—and two swivel bolt snaps. A swivel bolt snap is the snap found at the end of any dog's leash; it's the bolt that fastens the leash to the dog's collar.

Attach each end of the chain to a swivel bolt with the S-hook.

Squeeze the S-hooks closed with a pair of pliers. You now have an eighteen-inch chain with a swivel bolt securely fastened to either end. (See below.)

Make sure all parts are strong because a chain is only as strong as its weakest link. Do not use key rings in place of S-hooks; they will pull apart, they will break, and they are dangerous.

The eighteen-inch tether, stretched to its fullest length in all directions, then adding on to the tether the length of your dog, whatever he might be from end to end—let's say he is eighteen inches from nose to tail—this gives your dog lots of room, six

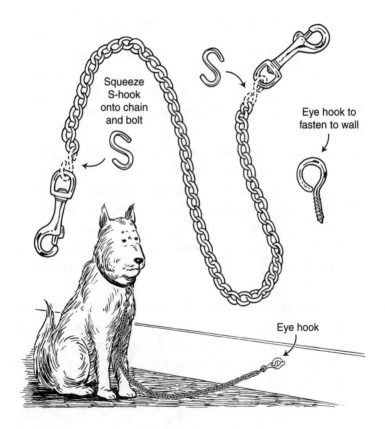

Squeeze
S-hook
onto chain
and bolt

Eye hook to
fasten to wall

Eye hook

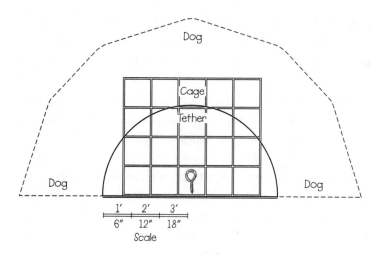

feet in length by three feet in width, and the height only limited by your ceiling. (See illustration above.) That's more room than any cage or crate.

If your puppy is a large or giant breed, growing by leaps and bounds, or if your dog is a large adult and still needs a tether, you might want to make the tether thirty inches long.

How to Use the Tether

Simply clip one end of the tether to your dog's regular buckle collar, *not a choke collar*. Take the other end of the tether and clip it to an eye hook you have placed in each of the spots you've selected to confine your dog or puppy.

Daytime

Tether your dog where he will be out of the way, but not out of contact with the rest of your household. You want him to feel wanted, you don't want him to feel left out of things and isolated. Make him feel like part of the family, part of it all; keep him around you. Remember you are imprinting this dog to you, not to a box or crate. That's the beauty part of this tether.

With the flexibility of the tether you can take your dog with you from room to room, wherever you have placed an eye hook. And you can put eye hooks anywhere.

When you go to work, leave your dog on the tether in a common area where he has light and a clear view. Don't tether your dog in a dark corner, a basement, or a laundry room. Nobody likes to be kept in the dark, in any way, shape, or form. If you want to leave music or the television on for him, make sure it's music he likes to listen to or a television program he enjoys watching. Your tastes in entertainment might not suit him.

At Night

Tether your dog close to where you sleep. Either by your bed, where he can see you and smell you, or close by and in plain sight. He is only tethered in the bedroom when you are there. Don't leave him tethered there by himself and go to work.

You'll be pleasantly surprised. Your dog will only need to be tethered here for a couple of nights until he learns to hold and picks up on a routine he can follow. Then, he can sleep in your bed if you want him there. If you follow our diet plan, you won't have any problems because it will be much easier for him to hold overnight.

With Company

If you want your dog with you when you go visiting, take the tether along. You can easily hook the tether around a chair, fastening it to itself, and then your dog stays by you. You won't have to keep an eye on him all the time and your hosts will also appreciate that your puppy explorer is not exploring their home.

Important

Use your common sense. Never put your dog near a heater or electric wiring. Don't put your dog near anything that can be a danger to him, or near anything of yours that he can do damage to. Make sure that your dog doesn't wrap himself around and get tangled up in the legs of a chair, a couch, or a bed.

Your dog should never be confined on a tether for more than six to eight hours at one time.

Outside

If you want your dog taught to go to the toilet outside, then get him out and teach him this right away. If you wait until he is fully inoculated, you could then have a problem teaching him to go there. He will be accustomed to going in your house, and you will have to break him from this habit and restructure a new one.

If your vet doesn't like the idea that your puppy goes to the toilet outside before he is fully inoculated, ask him over to clean the messes that the dog will be making in your house for six months.

Take him out, let him go to the toilet, bring him home, and wipe his feet off. Remember, you are taking your puppy out just to teach him where and when to go; this is not a play date, socializing time with other dogs or people, or any fun and games. This is pure business. So get business over with and get him home.

Inside—on Paper

Have the paper well away from his eating, sleeping, and tether areas. This place should be one you want to keep as his permanent toilet area. Take him off the tether when he has to go and put him on the paper. That's it.

What to Do for Mistakes or Deliberates

First get some paper towels and then get your dog. Don't say a word to him. *Do* not *call your dog to you and punish him.* Take him by his collar or carry him over to the mess and let him watch you clean it up. Show it to him, show him what he did. He knows it's his. Even if it's a week old. Give him a slap on the behind and chase him away. If he returns for a second act, you give him an encore.

If you are upset that you had to chastise your little one, if you are feeling really down on yourself, if you feel guilty for what you did, fight off the urge to scoop him up in your arms and tell him how sorry you are for what you did, and that you'll never do it again. Fight it off any way you can for at least a few minutes, before you heap all of this apologizing onto your puppy. He'll understand how you feel about him.

No matter how much you apologize to your dog, if he goes again, repeat everything. Your dog will quickly learn not to go in the house.

Get your dog on a schedule that he can count on, and that you will follow for his sake.

The Cardboard-Paper Match Trick

The dog's real mother teaches her puppies where and when to go to the toilet by licking their behinds. We wouldn't do that, we couldn't do that, you wouldn't do that, and we wouldn't ask you to do that.

We like to use a cardboard-paper match as a form of suppository. Although it really doesn't work that way. What it does do is stimulate the puppy and makes him want to push the match out in order to get rid of it. It doesn't hurt him; it is smaller than the thermometer that your veterinarian uses.

The cardboard-paper match is for your convenience. If your dog doesn't go on his own and you have to get going, match him. If one match doesn't do the trick, use more. If you make sure that your dog goes to the toilet before you go to bed, you'll both get a good night's sleep. Don't worry, your dog will not build up a dependency for the paper match.

You can put the match in your mouth to wet or lubricate it, if you want to, then pick up his tail and push the match in. But don't try to put the match in your dog first and then wet it. An anxious and nervous client once did just this. We thought we'd pass this piece of advice on to you, because it could be an embarrassing situation for you.

Food for Thought

Some people feed a fifteen-pound dog enough food for a fifty-pound dog and wonder why their dog is always on the move. Keep in mind that what goes in will definitely come out. Feed your dog the appropriate amounts of food for his age and size. Use your common sense when feeding. (See food chart.)

Length of Time on the Tether

The length of time on the tether changes with every dog. As he learns when and where to do his duty, you can give him more freedom.

Overnight is usually the best time to first try your dog free, for three main reasons: he will be in your bedroom, he will have gone before bedtime, and he will learn to sleep through the night, the same way you do. In two to three nights your dog should be off the tether in your bedroom and up in your bed where he belongs. During the daytime, depending on your dog, he should be off within four to six weeks.

Best of all, by your using a tether your dog will be bonded to you. He does not imprint to a tether—there is no physical way that he can—or look to run to a tether for security when he is frightened. There is no psychological draw for that. What he will do is run right to you for security, and that's the way it should be.

With traditional crate/cage housebreaking, dogs will be kept in these boxes for a minimum of two years, and some never make it out. And all become imprinted to these crates and not to you.

Baxter's List

Dear Paul and Suzanne:
This is the list of Baxter's problem behaviors that we sought help for from you:

1. *Bites us when playing with his toys.*
2. *Bites us when we are sitting on the couch watching TV.*
3. *Jumps on dining table and bites us when we eat.*
4. *Bites us when we tell him to get off the couch.*
5. *Barks and bites us when we cook in the kitchen.*
6. *Pulls when walking on leash and tries to eat the leash.*
7. *Eats paper and bites when we try to take paper away.*
8. *Grabs almost all small items in house (remote control,*

hairbrush, etc.) and chews them and bites us when we try to remove them.

9. *Runs out the front door.*
10. *Plays "catch me if you can" and hides when we try to get items out of his mouth (paper, remote control, etc.).*

Kenny and I want to take this opportunity to express our gratitude to you for teaching us how to live peacefully and happily with our four-month-old puppy, Baxter. In the two months since we adopted Baxter, he had grown increasingly aggressive. He was biting us several times a day. What started out as soft puppy bites when he only weighed six pounds worsened to skin-breaking bites at twenty pounds. His biting and aggressive behavior increased in intensity each week, and we were terrified of what his bite would feel like when he was fully grown and weighed fifty pounds.

Wanting to raise him properly and knowing that his biting needed to be stopped immediately, we tried the conventional methods (spray bottle, noise can, time-out in his crate, holding his mouth shut, pinning him down, choke collar, yelling "no bite") to try to stop his biting. None of them worked, and in fact he grew more aggressive with each day.

Both of us feared the worst—that Baxter was aggressive by nature and that he was unfit to be with humans. We have heard the horror stories and know that some aggressive dogs are put to sleep. We felt we had exhausted all the resources at our disposal, and our hiring of you was literally a desperate attempt to save Baxter's life. We read your book and knew that if you couldn't help us train him, then nobody could.

After just two and a half hours of working with the three of us, Baxter is a new dog. The aggressive behaviors he had ex-

hibited are completely gone. The throwing technique has allowed us to bond with each other. It has established a strong sense of attachment that is unachievable by using other training methods such as food reinforcements. Our relationship with Baxter is now parent to child instead of owner to dog. Perhaps the best part of your training method is that the results are immediate and do not require practice. Baxter would like to add that he enjoys not having to sit, sit, sit, thirty times a day. He is a model citizen and a true member of the family.

> *Very truly yours,*
> *Ken Y. and Jennifer K-Y.*
> *September 1, 1998, NYC, NY*

When a horse and rider are in sync, you have a winning combination. The rider is at one with his horse. Oneness, whether it's between people who are close to each other or close to their animals—their dogs, their cats, or other animals—all who are truly close, all who know each other well, have a magic communication, sort of a mental telepathy. That "I know what you're thinking and I know what you're feeling and I know what you're going to say, even before you say it."

This being at one with each other, this silent but strong connection, this emotional feeling, is what builds a caring, loyal friendship, a permanent bond. This is what life is all about. It's not about "sit."

When you and your dog and cat understand each other, when all the information is filtered through this understanding, it will be easier to see and discard all that doesn't make sense, no matter where it comes from, no matter how it's said, and no matter who is saying it.

Don't let obstacles—cages, crates, pinch and choke collars, muzzles, drugs, bad food, nonsensical information, or a slick bill of goods—come between you and your dog or cat. If you're teaching your dog to "sit," don't mistake it for the cornerstone of your friendship.

"Obedience without understanding is a blindness, too."
—From *The Miracle Worker,* by William Gibson

"The truth shall set you free."
—John 8:32

CHAPTER 8

The Origin and Evolution of the Penny Can

We believe it came out of Africa. And so it is to Africa that we turn our attention and curiosity for the elusive beginnings, the origin and evolution, of the penny can.

Many new discoveries are sometimes made purely by accident. This one was no exception. It was first tripped over, then picked up and examined more closely. The one who tripped over it, when he took a better look at it, as he turned it over and over in his hands, did he realize at that moment its earth-shattering possibilities and potential? Did this guy know what he had in his hands?

Today, penny cans are mere twelve-ouncers. Probably due entirely to modern marketing strategies and profit-making good sense. But way back when, way back, approximately four decades back, the discovered can we're talking about was much larger; it was a four-gallon can originally used for holding kerosene.

But the discoverer came up with a completely new way to use the can. An ingenious idea. He honed and perfected a secret technique, one that his society had never seen before or could ever have imagined possible. This discovery would be almost as important as the discovery of the wheel.

When the discoverer and now inventor of this new can technique adapted his can use, he changed the face and power structure of society.

Little did he know his moves would later be copied, imitated, and changed and not for the better. Changed merely for the sake of convenience, and adapted for modern man and woman, in their modern home, to be used as a tool, however primitive and ineffectual, with modern man's and modern woman's modern dog.

An evolutionary tool, the can constantly changed in shape, weight, and movement. A tool in the political power struggles between the three of them. The can became a leverage can. Ultimately it was an evolutionary dead end, a dud, a crushed can.

But before its dead end, this seemingly innocuous and unassuming can reached such great heights. It created such dependencies in so many, you seemed never to find an expert without one attached to his person. The can became the indispensable tool of choice for generations of dog experts, of every ilk, even though it was a dud. Man continued to use it for lack of a better idea.

Mike was the first and only primate, that we know of, to successfully use the can. Every other can used since then, especially those with pennies inside, inevitably fell short of expectations. Cans became the temporary answers to age-old problems. But they never worked.

Why, then, did the can fall short? Did it evolve too fast? Was the modern can too small? Were there inadequate amounts of pennies to be had, or were dogs just too smart to be snafued and hoodwinked by modern-man can shakers? We don't know for sure, but let's take a look at the origin, the evolution, and the use of the can, all the way to modern man. We'll follow the footprints in the sand.

Bang the Drums Loudly
. . . Mike's Magic Touch

He stood at a crossroads. His future hung in the balance. He looked across the clearing at the massive army that awaited him. All five of them. Their muscled, hairy arms, dangling from massive shoulders, touched the ground. Some lips puckered in war hoots. Some mouths opened, screaming for battle. Swaying back and forth, leaping up and down, they were a confident bunch, that massive group of five. Nothing could topple them from their perches of power. Nothing.

It was now or never. No turning back, a do-or-die situation, nothing to lose but life itself. His face was a study in absolute, intense concentration. His lips squeezed tightly, his eyes, like black coals, burned under his furrowed brows. He looked for any signs of an opening, for any advantage, any weakness, any chinks in the armor of the enemy. His ears were on alert, recording any and all sounds. His hands, tightly clenched, made the skin on his knuckles look as if it would split wide open. He was primed for the battle of his life. He was as ready as he would ever be. Mike was putting it all on the line.

But what had brought events to such an impasse? What had been the point of no return? Couldn't there have been some negotiations, some appeasement, some way out? Where were the diplomats, were they on vacation? Where was help? What had pushed Mike to take them all on, single-handedly?

Have you ever felt stepped on? Have you ever felt that nobody was listening to you? Do you always get the worst table in a restaurant, providing you can even get a table? Does it feel at times as if you're on the outside looking in? No one returns your phone calls, not even your mother? Do people kick sand on you at the beach? Does it seem like only the beautiful or the rich and famous get all the breaks in life? Most of us, at one time or another, have experienced this being-dumped-on feeling.

Consider the situation Mike was in. He was the most downtrodden, beaten-up, stepped-on, abused fella in his community. His balding appearance was caused by a bunch of local hooligans beating up on him and pulling his hair out by the handfuls. The poor guy couldn't sit down and enjoy a meal or even go out on a date and have a little fun, without being pushed around, day in and day out.

But you can only push someone so far and then they will either break down and accept their lowly status quo position at the bottom of the heap or fight back. Mike decided to fight back, enough was enough, he just wasn't going to put up with any more of this abuse. He was determined that things were going to be different from now on.

Mike needed a plan, he had to come up with an angle, something that would give him the edge in this game of survival of the fittest. Because he was up against some pretty tough customers. This guy was prepared to commit himself totally, in a do-or-die effort; in this winner-take-all society, any mistakes were generally final and could even be fatal.

What kind of an angle would give Mike an edge? The edge to cut himself a piece of the good life and the rewards that go with it. An edge so decisive that it would cut him a path to the very top.

This drama didn't unfold down in the Wall Street jungle of Manhattan. Nor did it play out in the wilds of the film industry in Hollywood. In these worlds, and other high-powered, cut-throat, nerve-racking environments, you can attain the edge you need simply by the cut of your suit or the cut of your hair. Your bulging wallet or your trophy collection of degrees and diplomas that decorate your wall will also trumpet to the world who you are and how seriously you should be taken. If that doesn't do it for you and you need more help, you can hire a public relations firm to tell everybody how great and wonderful you are.

All these things, and all this puffery, can help make the big man or the big woman. Or they can make the big man or big woman even bigger. If you still feel inadequate and that what you have is not enough, there's even more help to be had. You can get yourself a manager, an agent, a lawyer, a shrink, a stock-broker, or an accountant. Above all, if you're hungry, you've got takeout.

In Mike's Manhattan, none of the above ways-and-means stuff would cut the mustard. His jungle was the real McCoy. This hairy guy's world was a piece of the African wilderness. He couldn't use financial help, he couldn't use legal help, and psychiatric help, whether group or individual, was out of the question.

All the traditional trappings and tools that carve out a successful lifestyle for most would have been no help to Mike. There were no gray areas in his society clouding the issues of status and obscuring reality.

Mike had to change things all by himself, he had to stand on his own two feet. Being a realist, he knew there would be no help coming from anywhere at any time. He would have to count on a combination of brains, brawn, and a set of self-taught skills, skills learned the hard way, if he was going to make top banana.

Mike needed something. He needed an advantage, and by accident, he found one. To be more accurate, he tripped over a couple of them. Cans.

Most wouldn't see what Mike saw. Most would look and see only empty cans, but Mike saw more, much more. He saw the angle he was looking for, the edge he needed. The hook that would pull him all the way up to the top was right there. Right in front of his very eyes. And this, Mike saw in cans. A couple of empty four-gallon kerosene cans. Mike, this self-taught genius of the jungle, was going to use cans, he was going to beat his drum all the way to the top, to the top of his world, to conquer it.

Perhaps in another world, at another time and place, and as another species of primate, Mike might have been compared to the great drummers—Art Blakey, Max Roach, Gene Krupa, or Buddy Rich—and maybe he could have played with the great jazz bands and orchestras. But not Mike of the African jungle.

His immediate needs were much more important than just making wonderful music. They were political and military. His talents were focused in an attack mode. He worked tirelessly, perfecting sound and movement, creating his ultimate weapon. Having been oppressed for his whole life, he was now ready for war.

The battle lines were clearly drawn. He was outnumbered. His was not going to be an easy battle. The opposition was well entrenched and had had years to plan their defenses and strategies. It was a shame that kindness, as always in these situations, is mistaken for weakness. A policy of appeasement and diplomacy had gotten him nowhere; the more he gave them, the more they took from him, until he had nothing left to give, except what little hair he had left. Mike's desire for a peaceful existence had been totally run over and squashed.

His plan was about to be put to the test. He was going into action with his newfound Magic Touch, the cans, with which he believed he could beat his way to the top and drum out all of the competition. Any innocent bystanders would just have to get out of the way or suffer the consequences. After all, none of them had come to help Mike during his hard times.

There they were, the five of them. Mike's eyes locked on the boss. Imperceptible to all but the supersensed, the challenge was sent and received within seconds. There would be no backing down now, no retreat possible.

The opening volley was cast by Mike. He made himself as big and as mean-looking as he could. Vigorously banging, slamming, and hurling his kerosene cans, he charged the whole crew and attacked with a no-holds-barred abandon. They scattered. This gang of toughs who had previously kept Mike down, who had intimidated and beaten up on him for so long, split. Four now terrified big apes disappeared into the jungle, followed closely by all the panicked bystanders.

Mike continued giving it his all, he couldn't stop, because the leader, although shaken and stirred, hadn't totally given up. There was still plenty of fight left in this big guy. Mike kept it up, charging, banging his drums, throwing them, hurling rocks, and screaming, until even the big cheese threw in the towel.

The battle was over and when the smoke had cleared, it was obvious to all that Mike had won. He was now the champ of chimps. Established once and for all.

Now that Mike was sitting on top of his world, in complete command of his domain, that world, including his main rival, accepted him. Mike and his former antagonist became real good friends and grooming buddies.

Although the world went back to its normal social ways, if ever Mike saw any signs of anyone looking to break the peace and cause any kind of trouble, he would quickly put a swift end to any problems.

Mike's ambitious rise to the top was impressive. His creative use of the empty four-gallon kerosene cans and his total commitment to becoming the leader was observed, studied, and presented to the world by Dr. Jane Goodall and Hugo van Lawick in their book, *In the Shadow of Man* (New York: Houghton Mifflin Co., pp. 112–17).

From out of the jungle from whence it came, the can, many of them, now sit on top of your furniture, a temporary tool for modern primates to control their dogs in their own modern jungles, their homes.

The can, as it evolved, lost all of its powers. Once upon a time, long ago, in a special place, it did the job. But now, a shadow of its former self, it's only a crushed aluminum relic of the past, a shell, a little twelve-ounce shell, broken and taped, to keep pennies from falling out.

Complexes and the All-Encompassing, Problem-Solving Penny Can That Doesn't Solve Anything

Cans have a place in this world. They keep food from spoiling. If Napoleon had had cans to preserve food for his men when he invaded Russia, the Russian people might now be speaking with French accents. Andy Warhol became famous using cans as an art form. Street drummers use cans as musical instruments. Mike was able to use his four-gallon cans to help him rise to the top.

Cans are commonly used in language as in "He's in the can" or "He's going to the can." It also can be used as in "Can it," meaning "shut up," or in the case of peaches, plums, or pickles "can it" is to "preserve it." Can, can also be used as in something "can happen" or "can not happen." In the movie business, "It's in the can!" means the movie is finished at last. And when you go out for dinner and entertainment in Paris, you can see a cancan.

But cans shouldn't be used as the all-purpose problem-solver, the remedy to stop and cure everything that's wrong with a dog, all his negative behaviors, bad habits, mysterious complexes, and subtle syndromes.

Many trainers, experts, and behaviorists have built their whole practice around the pennies-in-the-can solution to cure everything from an acute separation-anxiety complex, fears and phobias, destructive bad habits such as biting, fighting, chewing, jumping, barking, and grabbing food from the table, to a myriad of other troubles both real and not so real.

Some use penny cans to such a degree that, if given the chance, they would recommend cans as a cure for the common cold. The fact is, the pennies-in-the-can-shaking business doesn't work; it is a Band-Aid on a problem, just a temporary fix.

In the case of an aggressive, biting dog, using the penny can could be a smoking gun. You might think that you have stopped your dog's aggression and your confidence will rise, but when you relax, when you let down your guard, that's when you could get bitten, twice as hard. It will happen when your dog realizes that the can amounts to nothing more than a noisy, harmless gimmick.

Beware of the expert who shows you how he shakes the can of pennies and, voilà, the dog listens. It works for him and looks impressive on television or in a demonstration, but after the shaker show is over, and the professional shaker goes away smiling with satisfaction and your money, you will be left shaking in anger and disgust when you find that the problems you tried to shake away are still there.

It seems that the temporary shaking fix wears off as soon as your check has been cashed. Your dog on the other hand might grow to like this shaker game and want you to do some more shaking. He might annoy you until you shake your can to his tune.

After all, just imagine how you look to your dog, standing there, shaking a penny can in his face. He is not going to be impressed. Even if you decide to shake, rattle, and roll every pot and pan in the kitchen, your dog might just decide to take a nap until you wear yourself out. Or, he might decide to bite you so you'll stop all the racket, come back to your senses, and stop giving him a headache. Then he will be able to continue with his important business, catching a few more winks, chewing a little more on the couch, barking a bit louder, practicing his jumping, or vacuuming the food off the table.

If after robbing a bank the thief ran and nobody tried to stop him except by yelling and blowing whistles, the robber might pause to see what all the noise was about, but there would be no reason for him to stop and give back the money. The next time he knocked off a bank, he wouldn't even pause because now he knows the noise doesn't mean a thing, it is no threat to him. He wouldn't take it seriously and he would keep on robbing banks.

However, if someone put a stop to him by physically taking some sort of effective action, then the story would have a different ending. The bank robber would be caught and put away.

It's the same situation with your dog. We're not saying he will rob banks or that you should call the police on him or put him away, but we are saying your dog will not stop doing whatever he wants to do no matter how much noise you make shaking cans.

Empty cans have only one good purpose today, and that is to be recycled. That's being constructive.

If you want something that works permanently, use the Magic Touch.

CHAPTER 9

Acute
Separation-Anxiety-Complex
Syndrome Psychobabble

Couldn't and Wouldn't

Rena was being driven crazy. Her two springer spaniels, Couldn't and Wouldn't, refused to be left alone. They barked and screamed incessantly every time she walked into or out of her apartment, with or without them. It didn't matter. This was annoying Rena, she was always on edge, her nerves raw from the stress of her noisy dogs and her angry, very vocal neighbors.

She called an animal hospital and engaged their expert behavioral specialist. He arrived at her apartment and carefully observed the dogs' behavior. He listened to their screaming as they were walked in and out of the apartment. He deliberated. He measured off the distance between the elevator and Rena's door, using his size 10½ shoes as rulers.

As if delicately walking a tightrope, he methodically put one foot in front of the other. He then added up the total distance he had measured off and divided the number by twelve. He explained to Rena that the distance is most important in these kinds of cases. He studied the dogs' toys. He wanted to know, which toy made them bark the most? Also, "Do the dogs bark more in the morning or does it build to a peak by evening? Does the barking subside by bedtime?" Their ages and their gender were important to him, and also where they had come from. He wanted to know what food Rena was feeding her dogs.

The investigation and the questioning went on all morning. Rena brought out coffee and lemon pound cake. This cake happened to be a favorite treat for Couldn't and Wouldn't, and with drooling enthusiasm they jumped on the expert to get the cake he was hastily putting in his mouth. And this behavior he also observed. With his mouth stuffed, he mumbled, "Don't let them eat cake." After swallowing his mouthful, he stood up and brushed the crumbs and the dog drool onto the floor. Pointing his finger at Rena, he strictly instructed her, "Never give your dogs people food. It's baaadd for them. It might add to their behavioral problems."

He mulled over all the information collected thus far, including the episode with the cake, taking notes and eating cake until the notes were extensive and the cake was all gone. Being a thorough man, he returned to the hall to make certain his calculations had been correct. They were; the distance was a good four feet from the elevator to her front door.

Leading Rena by the hand, he walked her into the living room and sat her down. The expert presented his findings: "You have two dogs with a classic case of acute separation-anxiety complex." Rena's brows went up, and her eyes opened wide at hearing the expert's opinion. Her immediate response was a horrified, stuttering, "Is-is it serious?"

The expert, not wanting to give up his moment of power and glory, decided to milk it for all it was worth. Rena, hanging on his every word, waited for the full, uncut version of this doggy doctor's diagnosis.

"Well," he said, "we've had success with this kind of problem in the past, but it's a long-term proposition. It will take patience, dedication, and lots of time and practice on your part, and I must come to see the patients and their progress two or three times a week to make sure you're doing everything right. If you don't follow my instructions to the letter, you could compromise the cure. These dogs don't want to be left alone. It seems they even have a great anxiety of being left alone. Classic acute separation-anxiety complex, if I ever saw one. And by the way, no more lemon cake for them, but, uh, would you mind giving me another slice, please?"

Before a shocked and worried Rena had a chance to reply, the expert, continuing to control the moment, reached into his black bag as if he were a magician pulling a rabbit out of a hat. But this expert's rabbit turned out to be a semicrushed soda can with tape over the openings and filled a quarter of the way up with pennies.

Smiling triumphantly, he shook the can with vigor. The dogs, who had been lying down, trying to relax and get over their trauma of being denied their favorite treat in all the world, a great-tasting, nonthreatening, mouthwatering, nontoxic, wonderful piece of lemon pound cake, now jumped up nervously and stared at the noisy object in the expert's hand, studying it and trying to figure out what it was.

"Aha!" said the expert, now shaking his head knowingly. "This noise, this shaking of the can, as you can plainly see, will be the catalyst of our program to desensitize these sweet but disturbed little doggies from their acute separation-anxiety complex and whatever else ails them."

He laid out his snake oil, his smoke-and-mirrors cure, along with a long rehab schedule. How many times a day and when Rena should shake her can. Including walking in the door with the dogs, walking out the door with the dogs, walking in and out of the door without the dogs, in fact, just shaking the can all the time. Rena was getting dizzy just listening to him. The barrage went on without a letup.

"This shouldn't take you more than a couple of hours at a time, four or five times a day, for two or three months. I also want you to put your dogs on our special designer dog food, Frankie's Formula—the Best, Brightest, Balanced, Most Wonderful, Healthy Dog and Cat Food Your Money Can Buy, and Buy, and Buy—or as we at the clinic call it, FF.BBB.MWH professional formula, for short. You can either pick it up at our clinic or we deliver for a modest fee. Make sure you mention my name.

"Don't worry. I will be checking on your progress two or three times a week. If this method of behavior modification doesn't seem to work, we will have to make adjustments. But don't worry. We'll handle it." He packed up, asked for his check, and left.

Rena practiced and worked at the program diligently, including the new food regimen. She even took time off from work. Three months went by. The only differences that she saw were that her dogs hated their new FF.BBB.MWH-professional-formula-for-short designer food, that she had many, many different kinds of cans of pennies in her house, and that her dogs seemed sad and depressed since they were deprived of their favorite, wonderful lemon pound cake.

One day Rena tried using quarters in the cans, thinking they might produce a new sound effect, because the old sound of the pennies in the can had long ago stopped working. But nothing, not nickels, dimes, half-dollars, or even silver dollars, worked anymore. It turned out that neither the denomination, the weight, nor the shape had any practical, aesthetic, or financial value or success. The cans were a flop.

What did not stop working was the expert, who kept showing up and billing her, showing up and billing her, and each time he came, he told her to practice more and more, and that whatever she was doing, it just wasn't enough, or that she was doing it all wrong. Everything was her fault.

He looked at her sternly. Maybe it was time for the big P or V? And that's not a designer dog food, it's Prozac or Valium. The expert declared, "These two are a couple of tough nuts to crack." At the mention of "Prozac" and "Valium" coupled with the "tough nuts to crack" crack, Rena began to view the future with a dismal eye and a nervous twitch.

She saw her dogs in the snake pit alongside a depressed and oppressed Olivia de Havilland, on a drug-addicted, ruinous road of no return. Good God, what would come next? Electric shock therapy? Rena begged the expert, please, could she at least give the dogs their last morsel of their favorite, wonderful lemon pound cake before they set off on their journey to hell?

The expert ignored Rena's heart-wrenching plea and said, "Don't be sad, don't fret, and definitely don't give them cake. If nothing works, I would recommend getting rid of Couldn't and Wouldn't. I have a cousin who happens to be a breeder, and he will give you two nice little dogs that Can and Will be perfect. Please mention my name when you call him so that he will make sure you get the dogs that will best suit your personality. I'll also talk to him and make sure that you get a good deal."

The floors of the entrance and the foyer of her apartment

were worn-out and would have to be replaced from all of the hours of therapy practice. The doors were destroyed by the acute-separation-anxiety dogs at their anxious best. Rena and her husband were arguing night and day because of this stressful situation, and their anxiety levels were going through the roof.

The dogs, however, remained the same with their complex intact and still sorely missing their lemon pound cake. However, the expert still felt confident that everything was going to work out just fine. He felt that way right up to the time Rena fired him and threw him and the complete coin-can collection out of the house, ending a lengthy, expensive exercise in futility.

Mental illness is a reality, a fact of life. The treatments range far and wide, and there are many qualified specialists to deal successfully with the various types of illnesses. Mental illness can range from mild, garden-variety anxieties to major, full-blown psychoses. Some are nonthreatening and some are downright dangerous. But it takes an experienced, well-educated doctor, who has spent years in rigorous study and practice, to diagnose and treat mental problems.

How can a veterinarian or animal expert, let alone a dog trainer, come up with a diagnosis of acute separation anxiety every time a dog destroys something, pisses on something, or barks his head off? And after making this diagnosis, the basic treatments are to say "no," "bad," "sit"; to walk a dog in and out of a doorway for hours at a time; to shake a can of pennies; to increase obedience training and socialization with other dogs; and keep the dog in a cage or a crate for years; and when all of this fails, the expert will then recommend Prozac or Valium. Jacqueline Susann could have written a sequel to her book *Valley of the Dolls* and called it *Valley of the Dog and Cat Dolls*, the way drugs are shoveled into dogs and cats.

Acute Separation-Anxiety-Complex Syndrome Psychobabble

Here's how we feel about the ubiquitous, all-encompassing "acute separation-anxiety-complex syndrome" excuse, which ranks second only to the "abuse excuse complex," which is also given as another reason for having more of that "acute separation-anxiety-complex syndrome!"

It goes like this. My dog, my cat, or even my goldfish must have been abused at some point in his life, before I got him, and that is the reason/cause for all of his behavioral problems and anxieties.

There are other reasons and rationales given for why a dog has or develops acute separation anxiety, and all of these reasons and rationales find a comfortable home under this one roof. Whichever way you choose to look at this complex, the only complexity about it is the complexity of reasons for getting it, and the mixed-up complexity of the experts who love to diagnose and treat it.

We know, and your common sense should help you see, that urinating can be territorial, it can be food-related, it can be a nervous habit, it can be bad manners, and it can be a mild form of aggression or even a urinary tract infection. All treated very simply. No acute separation-anxiety-complex diagnosis necessary.

Barking: A dog barks because he doesn't want to be left alone and knows that if he keeps on barking, you will come back to him. Not bad, good-thinking dog. Who wants to be alone if you don't have to be alone? Unless you like to be alone at times.

Other reasons a dog barks are to warn you of a dangerous situation, an oncoming disaster, an intruder, strange noises, just out of plain happiness, he enjoys being vocal, or he enjoys being a pest.

People act the same way, using words instead of barking to express these same actions and emotions. We guess some people do bark; those barkers might want to look into therapy of some kind. But for your dog, no acute-separation-anxiety-complex diagnosis is necessary.

Chewing problems are tied in with nerves and diet. If a dog has to get to the toilet and he's been taught to hold until he is taken outside, he will chew. And the more he has to go, the more he chews, until he can't hold anymore and then he goes to the toilet at his personally chosen area and stops chewing. Until he has to go again.

It's the same with us. When we can't get to the bathroom, we get a little nervous. We talk faster. We walk faster. We pace back and forth faster. Climb the walls faster. We might even chew on our nails, some gum, or on a pencil. But we have to get to the bathroom, and after we get to the bathroom, we calm down.

It's a damn good thing that when we show these signs of nerves, we are not tagged with an acute separation-anxiety complex and treated with Prozac when really all we needed was to get to the can.

To go to such dramatic extremes, to produce and direct this fantasy, to say that a dog who pees on your carpet, or eats your best shoes, your plants, or anything else in your house, or screams his head off when you leave, or annoys, bites, or attacks anyone in his domain, has a mental disorder, is pure fiction. This diagnosis belongs in the theater of the absurd.

How can one seriously state that all of the above are signs of mental illness to be treated with Valium or Prozac, or the shaking of penny cans? If your dog really did indeed have some kind of full-blown mental disorder, to shake a can of pennies in his face would be even more absurd.

Whatever the underlying cause or causes of his problems, your bottom line is still going to be the same: to stop unacceptable behavior. Using drugs or penny cans simply won't work.

There are approximately 60 million dogs and 60 million cats in this country. Can it be that every dog and cat that has chewing, peeing, or barking problems also has an acute-separation-anxiety-complex problem? You be the judge.

We felt that Rena's dogs were just a couple of spoiled brats that knew if they kept screaming and barking, they would get all the attention they ever wanted, and somebody to be with them all of the time. But once Couldn't and Wouldn't did listen to Rena, she spoiled them rotten, and you know with what. There is a difference between having dogs who behave like spoiled brats and spoiling your dogs rotten and giving them the world after they listen to you.

Rena followed our program and "cured" the "anxiety-complexed" dogs. It took her a few days to not only free the dogs from mental problems but also to teach them to come to her, to walk beautifully, and to housebreak them as well. She was pleasantly surprised at the wonderfully dramatic changes in the way her dogs looked and behaved while enjoying a fresh-food diet as well as delicious lemon pound cake. We call this diet our Fresh Food formula or FF formula for short.

All of the habits, good and bad, that a dog learns, he learns either by himself, by trial and error, or from you. If you socialize your dog with other dogs before he is solidly imprinted to you, then he will learn habits from other dogs. These are habits you are probably not going to enjoy.

If your dog develops any bad habits, they simply have to be broken and then restructured to suit you. A simple, no-nonsense process. Stop the bad. Encourage the good. Do not unnecessarily complicate your dog's life and your own with psychological gobbledygook that will prevent you from seeing the reality of what is going on and dealing with it.

In our opinion, the acute separation-anxiety-complex syndrome is only an all-encompassing designer slogan. It is the most widely used popular excuse, the few little words that cover all of the behavior problems your dog or cat might have or acquire.

CHAPTER 10

Trigger Points

The Tornado Trio

It was August. We were in the middle of a California heat wave with temperatures topping 112 degrees, a scorcher. The oppressive heat was so thick it was difficult to breathe. We stood wilting and waiting on the sidewalk in front of a split-level town house in Santa Monica, California.

The air conditioner in the car, no match for the heat, circulated nothing but hot air. Could it be the swirling hot air was a portent of things to come? After all, we'd been brought here, to this location, to stop tornadoes.

A powerful force emanated from the direction of the split level. One that could not be held back for too much longer. The house had been taken over by Mother Nature's all-powerful winds, tornadoes, three of them.

Inside, battling the elements, a director and his crew were

painstakingly filming the storm-weary couple, Lenny and Lisa, along with their three dogs, Diana, Elton, and Sly, otherwise known as the Tornado Trio.

This serious business had been going on for what seemed like an eternity. Finally, they finished the "before" sequences. Now it was our turn. We were signaled to come on up and face them, the triple tornadoes, head-on and do something never done before. Stop them. Stop them fast, and do it before we melted away in this sweltering desert heat. And most importantly, do it before lunch.

As we slowly climbed the steps to the second level, the door burst open and out flew a tornado, a spotted one. She was moving like the wind. Her mouth open, sucking up air to fuel the system, the red tongue signaling a warning, "Get out of my way." She could have gone even faster but for a very pregnant Lisa, who was anchored to the other end of the leash. Even the choke collar couldn't slow down this spotted speedster.

As the two of them, locked in their one-sided tug-of-war, tied precariously together by a tired length of nylon, whizzed by us down the stairs, Lisa forced a quick smile. "She's gotta peeeeee!" she cried out, as if this explained the situation and made it understandable.

We were unable to make out Lisa's next words, but as she disappeared around the bend, we believe she said something to the effect of, "I'lllll beee baaack in aaa miiiiinute." Looking at each other concerned, we sincerely hoped she'd make it to the bottom safe and in one piece, pregnant as she was and tied to a cyclone. She did. We figured that she must have been experienced in this type of dog walking.

Inside the town house, in the eye of the storm, we met a smiling, optimistic, although a bit frazzled Lenny, the hot and exhausted film crew, and of course the other two components of the Tornado Trio—Elton, the little fox terrier, and Sly, a mostly golden retriever. Sly was the baby and the largest of the three. The spotted, speedy speedster we'd met briefly in passing on the way up was Diana, the dalmatian.

The tornado is a powerful force of nature. These three storms had teeth; each one had forty-two, giving the winds a one-hundred-and-twenty-six-tooth force. That's heavy tornado force.

The amount of destruction that we saw in this house was no less than amazing. These three beauties had cut a swath so wide that not a piece of furniture was left unscathed.

A couch had been totally gutted and white puffs of stuffing lay everywhere except inside the couch, where the puffs were supposed to be poofing. A vintage chair was destroyed, along with cameras, shoes, cell phones, purses, and anything that wasn't hidden, taped up, battened down, child-proofed, or locked away.

The Tornado Trio had a particular fondness for all paper products, especially when the products were in the trash. They liked to take the paper products out of the trash and combine them with the puffs of couch stuffing. Excited and energized by the mess that all of this paper stuff and stuffing created, but not yet totally satisfied, the trio would then add toilet paper to the potpourri.

They dragged the toilet paper out of the bathroom, unraveling it, tearing it up, and strewing it as they flew around the house. This ritual, this homemade ticker-tape parade and paper storm of theirs, had become a major daily event.

Looking to catch squirrels, tornado Diana didn't let small obstacles such as windows stand in her way, she broke right through them. The door also showed evidence of tornado damage, after having been struck repeatedly by the trio's hurling themselves at it in frantic "Gotta get out of here!" attacks.

These attacks occurred anytime anyone went to the door

wanting to use it. In addition, the trio never stopped barking or peeing. The peeing also occurred anytime, anyplace, and anywhere, and apparently with no rhyme or reason.

Now we knew why it had taken so long to document all of this wreckage, this wrack and ruin, and these three wonderful culprits at work. As Lenny said, "It's always like World War Three exploded."

Lenny and Lisa had tried everything from praise and reward training techniques, to trainers, to training schools, to training books, to training tools. As for these "not-trained trained dogs" the evidence was in, and it was clear, nothing and no one had been able to control these twisters.

As soon as Lisa and tornado Diana came back, Lisa, hot and exhausted from the walk, plunked herself down on the half-eaten vintage chair trying to catch her breath. However, the intense heat had had no effect on these tornadoes.

Diana raced over to join the other two in a mad dance around the living room, including a couple of grand jeté's right over the couch, and all to the tune of the trio's nonstructured chorus of howling, barking, and growling at eardrum-shattering levels. They always did this after being separated, even if the separation lasted for only a second.

Over this din and confusion of flying feet and legs, the camera crew exhibited an admirable, stoic professionalism, as they struggled to position their cameras for the best angles and held high the microphone, so as not to miss out on any of these incredible sounds, now recorded for posterity, the natural sounds of a mad dogs' chorus.

Lenny shouted the obvious: "They're a little nervous and excited. Please don't pay them much attention or they might pee!" The director shouted something, it was difficult to make out what. The cameraman also shouted something and signaled to us, waving his hand.

As if we had heard the word *action* coming at us, we took it. Action. We grabbed up all the leashes and collars, held them up high over our heads, as high as we could, to keep them out of reach of the storm, because by picking up the leashes we had now drawn the attention of the wild ones toward us.

Jumping, howling, screaming, they came. These three thought they were going out and descended on us like whirling dervishes.

"The leashes are trigger points!" We tried to get out the words above the bedlam, to explain to the camera, for the benefit of a future audience, what was going on. It didn't matter. Nobody could hear us anyway. Nobody could hear anybody, anyway. And the cameras, trying to follow the action and confusion, had their own set of problems.

We threw all the leashes down on the floor as hard as we could. Bang! The dogs, the camera crew, the director, Lenny, and Lisa all froze. You could have heard a pin drop. The total quiet was a welcome sound. We then told the dogs how good they were for stopping the racket they were making and for settling down.

Turning to Lenny and Lisa, we repeated what we had said before, but which no one had heard due to all the deafening sounds the dogs had been making.

"The leashes are trigger points. When you pick them up, the dogs think they are going out and they go wild. And justifiably so. This has been the general pattern. But they don't have to go into a frenzy just because you pick up their leashes—whether you are taking them out or not. This pattern must be broken. Forcefully throwing down the leashes breaks it and neutralizes that particular instinctive trigger. The tornadoes now realize that there could be other reasons for leashes to be picked up."

Throwing down the leashes will get the dogs' attention. They will stop all their shenanigans, walk over, and examine them.

On the leashes is your smell, good or bad. The leashes have now become an extension of you.

Just think how much more effective a gavel-banging judge would be in an unruly courtroom if the gavel were thrown, instead of just banged furiously on a desk. Judges probably wouldn't throw their gavel at anyone in their courtroom. However, some must have thought about a good gavel throw from time to time, but instead they threw the book at those who needed it.

Everybody started to relax, including the dogs. Now Lenny took the leashes, and this time only tornado Elton started to show his spin and high-jump abilities, but only halfheartedly, testing to see if he really had to behave himself. He found himself singing and dancing solo.

Lenny threw the leashes down in his direction. All eyes were on Elton, and Elton, becoming self-conscious, walked over to Diana, sat down, and pretended to be bored. He yawned, gave himself a real good scratch, then stretched and plopped down as if that were what he had always intended to do. It was his way of saving face. This Elton the actor, giving one fine performance.

Tornado Diana was studying her toes, tracing the warp and the weave of the parquet floor designs with her nails. Young tornado Sly was studying the ceiling, apparently fascinated by the shifting, wavy patterns of light cast there by the heat and the camera lights.

Again, Lenny picked up the leashes and readied himself in case any of the tornadoes became active. And guess what happened? Nothing. Nobody barked, nobody jumped, and nobody peed nervously on the floor. Also, nobody got it on camera. Because everybody was shocked that this simple action had worked so well and so quickly. The tornado winds had run out of gas.

The leashes as trigger points had now been neutralized. No training or practicing was involved. A surprised Lenny congratulated his dogs for being so smart, learning so fast, and being so quiet. And for not peeing.

For the first time in this house, somebody other than the three dogs had finally asserted himself and moved up the social ladder a notch or two. This social mover and thrower was Lenny. He was now numero uno. He could even be the number-one tornado if he felt like it. He didn't, he's a laid-back kinda guy.

Another trigger point was the door. Picking up a handy paperback book, we asked Lisa to start opening it.

As the winds started to blow in that direction, we took the paperback and flung it hard at the door and in front of them. The book hit the door, the tornadoes stopped in their tracks, and we praised them for stopping.

We picked up the book and this time told the dogs to back up and get away from the door before throwing. We gave them approximately ten seconds to think it over. They didn't back up, but watched us intently. We threw the book at the door again and then the dogs backed away from it. We told them how good they were for doing that.

Lenny picked up a magazine, opened the door, and told the dogs to back away. They did. All in all, the door and the leashes as problems were over, and in just a few minutes without any training or practicing involved. Had the trio not stopped and continued to try to get out the door, Lenny was prepared to throw the book again and again, until the trigger point was neutralized, always keeping in mind that the object must be thrown in front of the dogs to make them back up.

For all the good work the trio had accomplished, we rewarded them with some great-tasting, healthy grilled shrimp and pasta. There is nothing like good fresh food. And there is nothing like a good meal after a hard day's work even if all of the hard day's work has taken no more than fifteen minutes, which was all of the time that we had taken to stop the tornadoes.

We suggested a change of diet from dry food to a combination of canned and fresh to stop the dogs from destroying the house and calm down. Once the dogs calmed down, then Lenny and Lisa would, too. The Magic Touch and the new diet changed things dramatically for the better.

To neutralize the door and the leash as trigger points:

Take the leash, walk around with it, put it down, pick it up, go to the door with it, open a window with it, take it in the shower if you want, sleep with it, but any time your dogs react wildly when you pick up a leash, throw it down hard.

The door:

Open it, close it, walk in, walk out, do all your door things. Carry a book or a sneaker while doing them. If your dogs react wildly, use the throwing technique: throw something at the door, you now know the drill.

In the kitchen:

If you open a can of food and your dog goes ballistic, the opening of the can is a trigger point. Take a magazine into the kitchen the next time you open a can. If your dog gets out of hand, throw the magazine right down. He'll stop. If he doesn't, repeat the drill until he does.

If you bring out your suitcases to pack for a trip and your dog goes into a fit of depression, lies down, and doesn't want to move, or if he runs and hides or even gets excited because he thinks he's going with you, the suitcases are trigger points.

For trigger points that cause wild behavior, you throw. For trigger points that cause a moping or depression type of behavior, give your dog something really good to eat. He'll perk up fast.

Three Good Dogs

January in New York. It seemed like déjà vu all over again, three dogs and a film crew coming over.

They rang the bell, as they've been taught, and we answered the door, as we've been taught. They were all surprised when the three dogs didn't come and help us answer the door or help us open the door or even run out the door when it was opened. These dogs have been taught not to do these things. The three dogs didn't throw themselves wildly all over the film people, they didn't jump up and down, they didn't bark, they weren't panting, drooling, or going stark raving mad. Because they have been taught not to. They have been taught to control themselves. They have been taught how to behave.

We were able to sit down in the library and have coffee, cake, and ice cream, all of us, all together, including the three white dogs, and oh, yes, that wild and woolly film crew. The three dogs were comfortably lying on the couch, relaxing and bothering no one. Because this is the way they've been brought up.

We gave the three little white dogs a bit of cake and ice cream from time to time. We gave each dog his own silver spoonful of ice cream, served from a Limoges china dish, because they don't grab, push, shove, or fight for it. So we don't need to worry about any breakage. They've been taught not to. They've been taught to wait, and they have learned that each will get his. No one will be gypped out of his proper share of ice cream and cake. They trust that the people they live with will see to it.

They don't have to take the law into their own hands. They ate what was given to them and left the other's ice cream alone. They didn't annoy any one of us either. No wolfing down their food and no begging from strangers. That's how they were brought up.

A cookie dropped to the floor. Tyrone the Handsome, the

youngest of the three dogs, the baby of the family, watched it drop. He thought no one would notice him as he nonchalantly, quietly, and unobtrusively slid slowly off the couch. He yawned and stretched. He then stretched his way over to the cookie, making every move in slow motion, becoming one of the longest little white dogs ever.

Of course all eyes were on the stretching, handsome, little white dog. "Leave it be and get back up on the couch." He did. He let it be and jumped back on the couch as if he had never moved in the first place. His face was the face of an angel, an unfairly accused, innocent one. He tilted his head sideways as if to say, "You didn't have to say that."

The two other dogs glanced at each other knowingly and smiled. Tyrone the Handsome had been caught red-handed in his surreptitious long-dog-stretching technique. We gave him the cookie for a good try, and a lengthy stretch. The other two dogs got cookies for nothing at all, just plain love.

This is a beautiful apartment, well furnished, well kept, and with plenty of precious antiques, rugs, and carpets. There are no dog damages in this house, no dog smells in this house, no crates or cages in this house, no gates in this house. These three little white dogs are free roamers, and these roamers get the best of their home environment. They are not treated as second-class citizens. Nor are they considered only toys or possessions.

Outside, the only restrictions these dogs encounter are the ones made by government. Restaurants, theaters, movie houses, and all other places that don't want these dogs around post No Dogs Allowed signs to let you know that dogs are not welcome.

In these situations, the dogs must become temporary fugitives from justice and have to hide quietly, camouflaged in unassuming carrying bags. They are then carried from one restricted zone to another by their chosen, two-legged, appreciative primates. You.

One of the film crew asked us if the dogs were not feeling well. Was something wrong? Why weren't they wildly jumping and bouncing around and begging for food as dogs do? Why weren't they barking as dogs usually do? Why didn't they do all of those doggy things?

These dogs have been taught manners. If there is going to be any barking or jumping when answering the door, they leave that wild behavior for the people they live with. If there is going to be any bouncing around, begging, or grabbing for food, they also leave that behavior for the people they live with.

These are two opposite mirror images. The California Tornado Trio didn't start out being wild, they slowly worked themselves up to that state. There were signs along the way that trouble was brewing. Nobody knew how to read the signs, and nobody knew how to stop the dogs at any point along the way. They were allowed to become wild and out of control.

The New York trio were brought up with rules and understanding. As members of a family unit, they were expected to behave as such. Every time a breakdown in communication or a problem surfaced, it was addressed immediately and taken care of.

Everybody learns how to behave, everybody is taught manners. Everybody learns rules. Dogs and cats are no exception; if you teach them manners, they have manners. If you teach them right from wrong, they learn right from wrong.

Although it's funny to see and hear about dogs destroying a house, knocking people down, or going wild and totally out of control, at what point does the laughing stop? When is enough really enough? We laugh because we can identify and because this is happening to someone else. We don't have to make the decision on whether the dog stays or goes. So it's easy for us to be amused. What about the dogs? The owner of the dog has to make this decision, and it is not so easy or so funny for someone to give up his dogs or cats. The excuse that this is the way dogs are supposed to be, or the way they always behave, is a lot of baloney. Dogs, like any other living, breathing creature with a brain, can be taught.

Lenny and Lisa love their three dogs and wouldn't hurt any one of them, not for the world. But one has to wonder, if they couldn't solve their wild-dog problems, would there be a breaking point? A point of no return? A point when they would give their dogs away?

Lisa was pregnant. The dogs were becoming a danger to her. Even though they were not bad dogs, not vicious or biting, by being so out of control they posed a real threat to her and the baby. In their wild state, one wrong pull, one wrong step, one wrong turn, or one wrong anything could be a blueprint for disaster.

If you have any disasters, man-made or natural, looming in your house, deal with them or go down in the storm.

CHAPTER 11

The Disillusionment of Central Position: Sibling Rivalry

Ripple Effect

Throw a rock in a pond, it makes waves. The ripple effect is put into motion. Anything new added to your life, a new family member, a dog, a cat, or a baby, makes waves. New relationships are not always predictable, nor are they always smooth.

Every ripple, large or small, affects the preexisting social structure. Not everyone looks forward to change. Some are very set in their ways and feel that change will disrupt and upset their smooth, stable lifestyle. Some are afraid of change and resist it. Others accept and look forward to what comes from the unknown ripples.

Rivalries can cut across species boundaries and show themselves in many different ways. Confrontations can be direct, but at least you know where you stand. You may not have solutions, but at least you know where you stand.

Then there are the manipulative, sneaky, underhanded ones, where you may never know where you stand or even realize what's going on until it is too late. And then you won't have a place to stand. Because the rug will have been pulled out from beneath you.

No one likes things taken away from him. No one wants to be left standing without a chair when the music stops. And many who have always been the center of attraction don't want to give up the spotlight. They want to keep the lights on themselves forever. At least until bedtime.

Social turbulence indicates a powerful force of nature at work. It shows up as sibling rivalry or the disillusionment of central position, depending on the age and relationship of the rocks in question.

Social Chaos:
Bachelor out of Paradise

He was mean, nasty, and out of control. As if that weren't enough, Felix the cat was also constipated, he hadn't gone to the toilet for weeks. Could that have been the reason for his anger and rage? Or, could sudden lifestyle changes, such as moving, marriage, or both, be the cause? Could it be he was confronting the disillusionment of central position? Or, was he expressing a powerful, straightforward, take-no-prisoners, territorial dominance? And what about that pernicious case of constipation, did that have anything to do with anything?

Whatever the reasons for Felix's personality disorders and this physical problem, his inclination toward a destructive, downward spiral could eventually lead to the end of Felix himself. For years, Felix had been a great cat and a terrific companion, but that paradise seemed to have been lost forever.

This six-year-old black cat and his human roommate, Oscar, had been sharing digs and a bachelor lifestyle for years without incident. Each had his own routines, and they shared chores equally, sort of.

Oscar paid the rent, their medical bills, he paid for their food, all the taxes, and everything and anything else. Earning his share of this partnership, Felix would, selfishly or unselfishly, depending on your point of view, get Oscar up early in the morning so he could prepare breakfast for both of them.

Furthermore, Felix would patiently listen to Oscar's in-depth philosophizing about life. Life's ups and downs, ebbs and flows, twists and turns, both past and present, and what lay ahead in the future.

Sometimes Felix would listen up close and personal; some-times, for a different perspective, he listened from a distance (another room), and sometimes while pretending to be asleep. Well, maybe he really was asleep. Oscar's conversations, long-winded and boring at times, could put anybody to sleep. Any-way, you could say, "They faced all of life's problems together, whisker to whisker, paw to hand, and tail to long-winded tale."

However, this peaceful bachelor coexistence was about to come to an end. Oscar fell in love with June. Oscar and June got married. June, Oscar, and Felix moved. They moved to a wonderfully spacious house in the suburbs, many times the size of their former city bachelor pad. You'da thunk with all that room and acreage everybody would live happily ever after. But noooooo waaayyyy. This was not to be. This created a rip-ple effect of boulder proportions.

Bigger doesn't always mean better. Although June and Oscar were happy with their new digs, Felix felt the town wasn't big enough for the three of them. No matter how big it was, it would never be big enough. This June bug was a thorn in his side. She would have to be put in her place, or go, or both. The latter option suited Felix just fine.

Felix was not about to be second or third on any social ladder, since for years he had been the uncontested top cat. He planned a complex and hazardous campaign, stalking, terrorizing, and biting June. Felix didn't realize that the stress of this undertaking would end up causing him such physical distress.

Generally, domesticated male cats, as well as domesticated male dogs, will compete with human males for the attention of all the females, whether they be human, canine, feline, or whatever other species you're bringing up socially in your household. But because of his longtime bachelor relationship with Oscar, Felix didn't quite follow this rule. In Felix's mind, he, and not Oscar, was the dominant male coexisting in this environment and always had been. Felix, at this point, saw June as a threat and chose not to have her in his territory unless he could control her. This was a classic case of the disillusionment of central position. This rivalry can occur with any species. No one likes to give up what's his.

Oscar and June were somehow going to have to deal with Felix. Felix's nasty new way of life had to be stopped. Maybe, Oscar thought, the constipation was making Felix mean?

Oscar, worried about Felix, went to his veterinarian for answers. The vet did everything he could do, including X rays and exploratory surgery. With the aid of medications, Felix went to the bathroom all right. All over the beautiful, pastel-colored, wall-to-wall, plush, brand-spanking-new living room carpet. This limited success was in reality no success at all. It was a medicated, temporary success. And no one wanted that kind of success deposited in the living room or any room.

It was like a merry-go-round. Oscar did his thing, he went back to the vet. The vet did his thing, he continued the treatments. Felix continued to do his thing, with a little help from the vet. And the bills did what they always do, they kept going up, up, and up.

Oscar explained everything in detail as he drove us out to his house. Even though Felix's physical problems were worrisome, and the thought of having to put suppositories and gels into his cat every day was a big pain in the butt for Oscar, as well as for Felix, the primary concern was Felix's vicious stalking of and attacks on June. It was becoming physically and financially impossible to keep him. Could something be done?

While Oscar was telling us his tale of woe, he reached into the glove compartment, took out a bottle of something pink, and had a swig of it. He said it was for his stomach, which had been giving him trouble since the start of all of this mayhem.

Changes in lifestyle can upset the best of us. You might be able to hide your feelings and disguise them successfully from people, but know with no uncertainty that your dog's and cat's senses are so highly developed, you'll never be able to hide anything chemical, which means emotional or physical, or maybe even spiritual, from your dog or cat. That's why the saying "You can run but you can't hide" goes double or triple or more for your cat and dog. They do key off and react to any changes in their owner's makeup. With all those incredible senses working in concert, we call it a veritable sixth sense.

Obviously, moving and marriage had affected everyone in one way or another. We explained to Oscar and June that moving can have incredibly negative effects. This is one of the most traumatic experiences for all of us animals. But our concern was for the health, happiness, and long life of Felix the cat.

June had a fresh pot of coffee waiting for us as she took us into the kitchen and sat us down at the table. She said, "I can't believe all this trouble we're having with Felix! Cats don't need anything, they take care of themselves. You're just supposed to put down their food, their water, and you clean the cat box once or twice a week, that's all. They're just cats after all." June swallowed two aspirin. She said it was for a headache that had been bothering her recently.

June's misinformed notions had to be straightened out. Cats, dogs, or any animals are not just things that walk around, eat, drink, and go to the toilet. They're living, breathing creatures that have feelings, can reason, and do interact in a family setting. As June found out, animals will respond in a positive or negative way depending on how they're treated.

We had heard their side of this story, but now it was time to examine the scene of the crimes and misdoings. This constipated, aggressive, and destructive cat had to get help. We're sure gels and suppositories have their place, but to place them in this place, to get the cat to go in the right place, was really out of place and proved not necessary.

The most obvious reasons for Felix's constipation were his food, the trauma of moving, and the marriage. But in addition, there turned out to be some surprising developments.

We went to see Felix's designated toilet area, which was in the laundry room, and heard some weird noises. At first, we thought it might have been the washer/dryer. It wasn't. Following the noise, we looked up at a small window near the ceiling and noticed a pair of dark eyes, a small black nose, and whiskers smiling down at us. It was one of the resident raccoons, who had probably been watching Felix trying to perform his duties. To the raccoon, this could have been a new form of recreation, like going to the movies. Even worse for Felix, when the raccoon saw him, he would excitedly pound on the window! This might have been entertainment for the raccoon, but for Felix it was very unsettling.

Who could blame him? How would you feel if you were so rudely interrupted during a very private and important moment and, especially, saw a face you'd never seen before in your life staring at you? Even if you knew the face, it would still be unsettling.

Felix, being a city cat, had never seen a raccoon before. Living in midtown Manhattan, the closest thing to a raccoon that Felix had ever seen was the full-bearded psychiatrist with the dark glasses who lived next door. But even he never peeked at Felix. What was he to do? What was he to do?

This could easily have been another reason why Felix became constipated. This was emotionally disturbing for Felix. If he couldn't go in his litter box, the only place he had always gone, and he didn't have any other place in the new house to go, he didn't know where to go, and so he didn't.

Generally speaking, when one goes to the bathroom, a magazine or a newspaper is taken along for the ride, in order to relax. Poor Felix. He could never relax. He not only had to contend with the raccoon outside, staring, scratching and pounding, but also with the rhythmic beat of the washer/dryer on the inside. That would be enough to cause concrete worries for anyone.

Finally, in this combination laundry room/toilet/peep show were his food and water dishes. This made it a full entertainment center. Oscar and June, not knowing what else to do, had started locking Felix up in here. Maybe this was the solution? But in reality this lockup made Felix even more bitter and blocked.

All houses, homes, and apartments have dining rooms and kitchens. We're not saying that Felix should have his own dining room, but his food and water, for sure, should never be in or near his toilet. His food and water should be in the kitchen and his toilet should be somewhere else entirely.

Moving, marriage, being locked up, the toilet and feeding area in the same place, the raccoon staring and banging on the window, the noise of the washer/dryer, the disillusionment of central position, aggressive competition for territorial dominance, any one of these disturbances could have felled the biggest of oak trees, let alone a small, but important, family member, Felix the cat. But to have encountered all of them, all at once, was guaranteed to cause upheaval and a purr-fect, cat-a-strophic cat-astrophe.

Changing the type and quality of Felix's food, regulating his feeding times, separating his dining area from his toilet area, and finding a more suitable bathroom for him cured his constipation and redirected Felix to his litter box. With the food change, the constipation was over with within a couple of days.

Stopping Felix's aggressive behavior was simple. We taught Oscar and June how to use our Magic Touch. This technique is tailor-made for stopping aggressive cats or dogs.

A major reason why people can't or won't try to stop an aggressive animal is because they themselves could get hurt. Our Magic Touch will keep you out of harm's way.

Since Felix wanted June out of his life, he harassed her continuously in every part of the house. Day in and day out. But the main attacks were happening in the bedroom.

Probably because that is where Oscar and June spent a lot of time together, and they would lock Felix out of the room when they wanted privacy. Felix didn't like this, he didn't like this treatment at all. He had never had to put up with this type of no-cats-allowed stuff in his New York apartment.

Felix, scratching and biting, would chase June into the bedroom and zip inside before she had a chance to shut him out. Sometimes, June would throw herself under the thick bed quilt for safety. But the minute she looked out, to see if the coast was clear, there he'd be, waiting. Camped out on top of the quilt, growling and hissing at her.

Since the bedroom was the main confrontation area, that's

where June confronted him. It didn't take long. The minute June went up to the bedroom, Felix confidently followed her. He enjoyed this intimidation game. But this time June had a pair of sneakers with her.

When Felix started in with his aggressive nonsense, he got the surprise of his life. It would have been enough of a surprise to have solved the constipation problem, if that had not already been taken care of.

Felix hissed, growled, and started to go after her. June threw a sneaker at him. It hit him. It stopped him in his tracks. Felix jumped. When he landed, he checked out the sneaker, then gave June a look of disbelief. He settled down and thought things over.

June got ready to throw the other sneaker, should it become necessary. She told Felix to get out of the bedroom and cocked her arm to throw again. He left. The confrontation was over with.

For several days June stayed on alert, just in case Felix had a memory lapse. But he didn't. However, June had the security of knowing what to do and how to control this cat.

Besides being a tough cookie when she had to be, June spoiled Felix rotten. He became her cat, they were inseparable. The Oscar connection was now over. He was the third party, the other guy in the house, third in the pecking order. Oscar didn't mind being the third party. He was just happy that things had smoothed out, that peace had come to their part of the burbs.

We were happy that this peace treaty had been reached. Felix the cat was now destined to be around, to become an old, happy Felix the fat cat.

The agreement was signed with fresh peppered turkey, a big bargaining chip in the beginning, but now one of the main staples on Felix's new menu, along with tuna, salmon, assorted vegetables, and carbohydrates. As well as the occasional steamed dumplings from Hunan—the restaurant, that is.

Felix had mistaken kindness for weakness, but the Magic Touch had rectified this error in judgment. Once you are given the right information, it's real easy. There was no training involved. Nothing was practiced, everything was solved quickly.

CHAPTER 12

Aggression

Mouthful

Aggression is "politics with bloodshed."
—Mao Tse-tung

"A Way with Animals," Shaken to the Core

Dave went to visit a friend he hadn't seen for some time. His friend had a dog, a shepherd-collie mix, and she seemed to be a happy dog. Dave, although he had never met his friend's dog, felt comfortable around animals; he felt that he had "a way with animals" and that all animals liked him. He decided to make friends with this friendly dog.

But just as quickly as this happy, friendly dog became happy and friendly, that's how quickly she sank her four largest teeth into Dave's arm. Dave painfully felt that this was not a happy and friendly thing, for his friend's friendly dog to do.

The dog on the other hand, sure looked happy and friendly while doing it, happily wagging her tail behind her, as if she had thoroughly enjoyed putting those four friendly holes into Dave's arm.

The dog's owner gasped in astonishment and told Dave, "I'm terribly sorry, my dog has never done this before. She's never nipped or mouthed anybody. What did you do to her? You must have done something to provoke her into doing this. She is always such a happy, friendly dog."

Dave's confidence and belief in his "way with animals" was shaken to the core. All gone in one friendly, happy, dedicated bite. He had been bitten to the reality that his way was, for sure, in no way a good way.

It took Dave a long time to put his hand out in friendship to another dog. He couldn't forget the way the dog had responded to his friendly greeting. He couldn't get over how this friend of his, the owner of the dog, had acted. He had immediately blamed Dave, and not the dog, for this nasty bite.

Then, adding insult to injury, this person had come up with the lame excuse that his dog had never bitten anybody before, just maybe a little nip here or a mouthing there. But there had never been a true biting incident, ever.

This was a trust broken. Dave might trust someone to tell him about an interesting book, a good movie, or the weather; even if the information turns out to be wrong, there's no harm done. He'll either be bored or get wet.

But he won't blindly trust someone's interpretation of what constitutes a happy, friendly dog anymore, because erroneous interpretations might easily put him in harm's way. Once bitten twice shy. Twice bitten, who knows?

Just because a dog wags his tail and looks friendly doesn't mean a damn thing. You can still get bitten. Even if you feel, as Dave used to feel, that you have a "way with animals," you better make certain that your "way" is agreeable with the animal you're looking to have your way with.

Even if you feel you're a "whisperer," better whisper from a distance; speak softly if you like, but also carry a big Magic Touch.

There is so much misinformation out there, and there are so many excuses made, and there are so many reasons and so many nonsensical ones that owners and experts will give for biting, that the truth gets clouded over.

Many people get bitten by the dogs that they are assured don't bite, never bite, wouldn't think of biting, or have never bitten anybody. But still, at the end of the assurance tale, they get bit.

Keep in mind that a biting dog, by any other name, is still a biting dog. If a dog learns that he will get his way in every and any which way by biting, then his path to success will be in more biting, harder biting, faster biting, and in his mind, the best biting that he can do.

It is no different from a person in business who finds the keys to success. He will keep on doing what works, for as long as it works, and he will improve on what works if he can, until he is stopped.

This was a dog who had learned how to bite and had become successful at doing it. This was a dog owner who wouldn't face up to the reality that his dog was a biter. Instead, he preferred to put the blame and responsibility on those who were bitten, and he made excuses to cover up the problem instead of stopping his dog from biting.

Had he stopped his dog from biting when it first started, when the dog was young, it would have been easy to do. But then he, and everyone else, found the nipping and mouthing cute and thought it was natural puppy stuff. If it had been called biting from the beginning, then it would have been treated as biting and stopped at the puppy stage. A biting problem, if not stopped immediately, will grow along with the puppy, until you have a full-grown dog with a full-blown bite.

Nip the nipping and the mouthing in the bud, as they are more often than not the prelude to a good bite. When the dog sinks his teeth into your arm, it is a bite. A nip is a drink, a bite is a bite. If your dog is a nipper, it could mean your dog likes to take a few drinks. If your dog closes his teeth around your hand or leg or behind or whatever, he's a biter and he should be stopped from taking these mouthfuls of you or anyone else.

According to *Webster's Collegiate Dictionary*, tenth edition, *mouther* means one who likes "to move the mouth especially so as to make faces." And *mouthy* means "excessively talkative." So if your dog is a mouther, it means he makes faces. And if he's a mouthy dog, he talks excessively. If someone tells you that his dog is a mouther or a nipper, be careful. Chances are you're going to get bit, not mouthed or nipped. Unless, of course, the dog really is a nipper; then you might find yourself being invited for a drink. And if the dog is truly a mouthy mouther, you better be prepared to be listening to a garrulous talker or a face maker, while you're having that drink.

You are not always to blame if you are bitten. And it is not always the dog's fault or the cat's fault either. However, once a dog or a cat develops these biting habits, the way to stop them is with our Magic Touch. It keeps you out of harm's way and tells your dog or cat in no uncertain terms to stop.

The Red Knight

No one visited the town house anymore. The only people who dared show up were those who were paid to: plumbers, electricians, meter readers, the phone company, the cable company, and anyone making deliveries, including the mail.

Even they were reluctant visitors. This address was not for the faint of heart. All who entered had to face Red Lancelot. He exacted a price from any and all who crossed his path. What price fear? This network of necessary maintenance personnel carried word of his exploits far and wide. Thereby making the visitors' list an extremely small one.

The Red Knight was big, ninety-plus pounds. With his flashing, swordlike canines, this red Doberman dominated not only the round table in the dining room, but also the rest of his domain, this four-story town house set in the West Sixties. He terrified all those who came, who fled quickly, and those who adamantly refused to come back.

The title to this piece of Manhattan real estate belonged to Melissa, but Lancelot couldn't have cared less. She might have owned this house, but as far as Lancelot was concerned, he and he alone ruled supreme. He left his royal signature on many an arm and many a leg. For those who feared to face him, for those who turned to run—these he nimbly caught, leaving a permanent impression on their buns.

The other woman in Lance's life was Morgan, the weimaraner. When she spoke, he listened. When she wanted to eat, he stepped aside. Whatever Morgan wanted Morgan got. A quixotic gal with unstable moods, Morgan cast a spell on the unsuspecting, lulling one into a false sense of security, a gooey, dreamy state of being.

She did this by plopping her head on your lap and lazily gazing up into your eyes. She quickly sized up the measure of the mark, you. She always knew when she had a patsy in her paw; it was when the patsy turned to mush under her mesmerizing gazes. Morgan's stare went so deep, was so penetrating, that few could resist her hypnotic and intense eye contact. The patsy, as all patsies before, felt flattered by Morgan's interest. It gave the patsy a feeling of a mysterious kinship with all animals. But the truth was, Morgan's penetrating gazes were not penetrating gazes at all. They seemed so because Morgan was almost blind in one eye and had to cock her head sideways on the lap in order to see anything at all.

Once she had you all wrapped up in her cozy quilt of charm, she would suggest a quiet walk, just the two of you. A walk, to stretch the legs and take the air, a walk along the steamy sidewalks of New York.

And there, on the street, this spellbinding eye gazer, this five-year-old people charmer, turned into a holy terror. Morgan hated dogs. Especially large dogs. She would fiercely attack and terrorize them all. Even friendly large dogs, just out for a quick sniff 'n' pee, got the scare of their lives and, if not hastily removed from the scene, could end up as grist for Morgan's rampaging mill.

Melissa called in a behavioral expert, and not the first expert in a long line of experts and trainers, to try to stop her Lancelot from attacking and biting people and her Morgan from attacking and biting dogs.

Previous experts and trainers had come armed to the teeth, with chokes, muzzles, prongs, head and neck turners, electrical equipment, and all sorts of other contraptions, but all to no avail. One trainer in Paris even wanted Lancelot dead and replaced. Melissa got rid of this expert real fast.

Now a new expert arrived. He walked in. He came face-to-face with the Knight. He shook his penny can. He got bit. With a bloodcurdling scream, he ran out of the house terrified, after his first and only line of defense, his penny can, proved to be no match for Lancelot's straight-on, teeth-chomping, tail-wagging, speedy moves.

This latest in the line of experts, this newest notch in the Knight's belt of dubious honor, left, thanking God for the timely and successful slamming of the gate behind him.

After conceding the East Coast to Lancelot, this expert is now expertly shaking cans in Los Angeles. A bill arrived a week later from the bitten expert for services rendered. Lancelot ate it as it fell through the mail drop. He deposited it on the street a day later; it was picked up, bagged, and put in the trash.

Melissa asked us, should she crate, leash, or muzzle her Knight before we came over? These were the only ways she knew to restrain him when people came to the house. "No, loose the Knight, let him go, let him challenge us. This knight-errant stands little chance against the Merlinesque Magic Touch. We thinks, we hopes."

We explained to Melissa that if the dogs were to be taught not to rush the door when the bell rang, and Lancelot not to bite anyone coming in, then the problem had to be faced head-on. The way it would normally unfold. And that's without any re-straints or leashes on the dogs. If leashes or restraints are used to hold back the dogs, how can the attacking and biting prob-lem be addressed and stopped? It can't. You have to let them do what they will, so you can stop it. If not, then you will have to tie your dogs up forever, and they will always attack, and Lancelot will always bite people whenever he's free. Remem-ber, to err is human; one day you will err and forget to lock your dogs up.

We rang the bell, the dogs went into action. They crowded Melissa at the door and barked with eager anticipation, anxious for us to come in. Salivating, licking their chops, waiting for a chance to dig their teeth into this situation.

Melissa nervously unlocked the door and then stepped aside. We pushed the door open swiftly, with some force, backing the dogs away, so that we would have enough room to use the Magic Touch technique.

As we started to come in, they came at us. We threw hard and fast and with good aim, because if the Red Knight was going to bite us and show us how tough he was, we could do no less and our aim had to be true.

At this stage, at the beginning, you get only one chance, one shot. We threw our keys and a big hiking sneaker. This shocked the dogs because they had never experienced anything like it before. Their hesitation allowed us to get inside, but it didn't last for long. They recovered quickly. Backing up some, the dogs continued barking, trying to intimidate us, but for the first time you could see that they weren't so sure of themselves.

Morgan, still barking, walked over and stayed by Melissa. Since Lancelot wasn't yet totally convinced that he couldn't push us around, he continued his threatening posture. We threw the hiking sneaker at him again. Both dogs eyed us with suspicious uncertainty but stopped barking.

We walked in and picked up our keys, a magazine, and that invaluable tool, the big sneaker, just in case. Morgan, sitting next to Melissa, was now starting to relax. But Lancelot still stood his ground. This time we only tossed the magazine near him. It worked. The attack was over.

Lancelot smelled the magazine, and pretending indifference, he turned, a bit ruffled, but no worse for wear, and walked away to the farthest part of the room, lowered himself slowly to the floor, and watched us from there.

Now with some breathing room and feeling much more comfortable, we could sit down and explain to a surprised Melissa what had just happened in this fast-moving drama. The whole episode was over in less than five minutes. Melissa told her dogs how good they were for leaving us alone and in one piece. Morgan, at her charming best, came over to greet us and probably to get a better look at us.

Melissa, now following our directions, threw a small magazine over at Lancelot and called him to her. As you all know by now, you must teach your dogs to come to you first and foremost. He didn't move. Melissa, without hesitating and without saying a word, went and got him by the collar and pulled him over to the table from where she had first called him. She praised him, told him to lie down, and he did. The next time she called him, he came. No problem.

We explained to Melissa that we threw initially so we could get into the house safely. But from now on only she, and no one else, should ever throw at her dogs, because the throwing technique is a powerful tool.

These are your dogs, you control them and no one else. We coached her through the use of the Magic Touch again, until she felt confident that she knew what to do.

When the bell rings, if the dogs aggressively rush the door, take a magazine and aggressively throw it at the door and at them. Then go to the door. Do not call them. Pick up the magazine. The picture should look like this: the door, then Melissa, and the dogs well away from the door.

If the dogs are at the door, throw the magazine at them again and continue to do this until they get the message and get away from the door. It is that simple.

Pick up the magazine and open the door. If the dogs start coming, turn around to them and throw your magazine at them. Tell them to go away, chase them. You continue this drill until the dogs have stopped charging and go away from the door.

Now, you can bring your company in. If the dogs run over to threaten your guests in any way, throw. Let Morgan and Lancelot know these are your guests, not theirs. And the guests are allowed to come in safely, without being tattooed with teeth marks.

We went outside, rang the bell, and let Melissa handle it. She did. After a few times, the dogs didn't even bother to move or bark when we rang the bell and walked in.

If you want your dogs to bark a few times for security, then let them bark a few times, tell them that's good, and then tell them it's enough and to be quiet. If they don't stop, throw. They will learn to bark the amount of times you want them to. They will learn to stop barking when you ask them to. No problem.

Melissa wanted to see how her dogs would react if we sat down and had something to eat. Generally, they wouldn't allow people to eat in peace at the round table. They would bully, push, grab, jump, bite, and growl and just scare the hell out of everyone.

This is the other reason they were always tied up or put away. We went one better. We took the parmigiano-Reggiano and a nice ripe Gorgonzola and put them on the floor. We did this over Melissa's frantically emotional objections; she expected a feeding frenzy. The frenzy turned out to be a fizzle.

Lancelot didn't move at all. Morgan meandered slowly over to the cheese, Melissa dropped a travel brochure in front of her, and Morgan stepped away and slid down next to Melissa. Then Melissa gave both dogs some of this good cheese for being such good dogs. That's how to do it: spoil your dogs rotten when they behave. Give them everything when they behave.

Whenever we're working with people with biting dogs, the emotions on the table are apprehension and fear. What about fear? If you are frightened or apprehensive, it shows. It shows in a big way, because sight and smell are two of the dog's or cat's supersenses. What are you supposed to do? You can't always control these strong feelings. Will it affect the dog's behavior? Won't he know you are frightened and would you then get attacked and bitten? How do you handle this fear?

Good questions. Fear not. You'd smell the same way to Lancelot, or to any dog, in fear or in anger. When you are frightened or angry, the adrenaline is pumping through your body. Salt and nitric acid, better known as perspiration, pour out through the pores in your skin by osmosis. The more frightened or angry, the more sweat.

That's the scent the dog and the cat pick up. To them, you've just lit up like a lightbulb. If you step back, they know for sure it's fear. These masters of the scent. If you stand up straight and hold your ground, they're not so certain. These masters of the body language. But, if you step forward and throw, then they will be the ones to back up and back away.

These masters of the scent, body language, and teeth are still masters, but now they have been introduced to the secret that only primates hold, how to throw. You are now a master in your own right. This introduction to the Magic Touch will remain a puzzle to them forever.

They will never be able to duplicate, get around, or beat it. You are now the dominant species coexisting in this environment. You are in charge. Consider this a new social order.

It had taken two or three throws for the Red Knight to get the point. Once gotten, he had retreated to the back of his castle, to the farthest corner of his realm, to give himself time to figure out what had happened, what we had done, how we had done it, and how to get around it. If he could put it together and sort it out, then he might once again be able to be the big bully of yore. The Red all-conquering Knight.

He won't be able to figure it out. He will never figure it out. Since Lancelot is not a primate, he can never learn to throw.

Whereas Lancelot had managed the interior of the realm and kept that under the control of his paw, by menacing the entire services network and those few who came to call on Melissa, Morgan did the terror management on the lands surrounding the castle in the West Sixties.

This arrangement of power had come to pass because the

two dogs hadn't trusted Melissa with their security and had become aggressive. They had taken security matters into their own hands. Even though there were no security issues.

When Melissa brought the Magic Touch into play, the power structure rapidly changed shape. Both dogs now saw Melissa in a new light. No longer being a mere powerless puppet, pulled along by a couple of canine puppeteers, Melissa had exhibited some real brass, she wielded real clout from that moment on. She, a senior citizen, with a Magic Touch supersense, a new force to be reckoned with. And now, this senior was prepared to stop Morgan from fighting with dogs on the street.

Morgan terrorized other dogs in the outside world for many reasons: maybe her partial blindness, maybe not trusting Melissa, maybe early play fighting, socializing with other dogs, and so on and so forth. But these reasons were immaterial. The problem still had to be addressed and stopped, and not with a bunch of excuses. Excuses are a prelude to a final dog giveaway.

Melissa had an advantage in these confrontations now because she had already shown Morgan the Magic Touch side of her personality. She had the advantage because she knew what Morgan would do when Morgan saw another dog. But Morgan wasn't so certain anymore about what Melissa would do. The being-taken-for-granted scenario was now reversed.

Morgan took a chance anyway and went after a dog. It was quickly stopped by a determined toss right on target. A second dog appeared and Morgan looked at Melissa. Melissa told her, "Don't even think about it." She didn't. This confrontation was over before it began. Melissa didn't wait for bodies and teeth to make contact; she made her moves fast and direct.

Don't wait for an attack to happen. Go into action as soon as your dog shows interest in another dog.

The clues of interest look like these. The ears muscle up, the tail tenses, the body gets bigger than you've ever seen and stiff as a board, and the hackles on the dog's back stand up at attention. Your dog looks like one huge, wound-up spring. These are all the signs to alert you and let you know when you have to take action. Don't wait to see them all, seeing one is enough.

Some dogs, being successful street fighters, don't show any signs. They just go right at it. These are the real veterans. They know what to do and where to grab. Just like professional fighters. In the case of veteran street fighters, you still have an advantage, because you know your dog is looking for a fight. Go into action when either you or your dog sees the other dog. If you're wrong, you can apologize later. Chances are your instincts have told you right. Being forewarned is being forearmed.

Another way to stop a lunging dog is to continuously snap/jerk the lead hard until your dog stops. You can only accomplish this if your lead has some slack to it. Not much, but some. Those with aggressive street fighters tend to hang on to the leash tightly every time they see another dog. This only alerts your dog to get ready for some action. But even still, the Magic Touch works better and is our choice.

Outside, the difference in Morgan was immediately apparent and Melissa was pleasantly surprised. The Magic Touch worked quickly because Morgan had been introduced to it in the house first. She had learned mostly by watching the schooling of the Knight. This next step for her was just a course in continuing education.

We believe that the Red Knight, actually a very sensitive dog, became aggressive by being kept in a crate, kenneled with other dogs, and because he was trained in an aggressive, heavy-handed, tough manner.

Kenneled with and imprinted to other dogs, he grew up

trusting dogs, but not people. When Melissa had gotten him, he was already nine months old and his main behavioral imprints were formed. He was a frightened dog around people, an unpredictable fear biter.

He learned to accept Melissa in time because she posed no threat to him in any way, but he didn't trust her with his security. When he was alone with Melissa, he was perfect. In a world full of people, he was unpredictable.

When you are working with a large, sensitive dog like Lancelot, you want to be firm and direct, but when he is responding to you, you must be superindulgent and sensitive as well.

Putting a dog in a crate is not sensitive. Putting a choke or a prong collar on your dog is not sensitive. Putting a collar on your dog that twists the head or neck is not sensitive. Neither is putting a muzzle on his face.

And to put a dog such as Lancelot on tranquilizers or Prozac, which he had also been subjected to, could cause major problems and did. As you know, mood-altering drugs have caused violent reactions in people, and they can in dogs as well.

The strong procedures that we initiated with Lancelot and Morgan put us in a position to restructure their nasty and aggressive habits and gave Melissa a way to control her dogs from then on, with just a small magazine or even a pair of socks. Soon, she was able to control them verbally, but she would always have her state-of-the-art backup system when needed, a Magic Touch.

Melissa, enjoying the rest of the summer in France, called us from the French Riviera to tell us about her new and wonderful Lancelot. Her first pleasant surprise happened upon her arrival.

The refrigerator in her home was broken and had to be immediately repaired. The broken refrigerator wasn't the happy surprise. It was when the repairmen came in to fix it; much to everyone's amazement, Lancelot left them all alone.

Melissa went on to tell us how her Lancelot was now a *chien célèbre* in all the patisseries in town. It seems that everyone loves to give this sociable party animal hugs, kisses, croissants, baguettes, *croque-monsieurs,* and crepes. And furthermore, this well-fed, friendly Doberman listens to his newfound friends in French as well as other languages.

After all, delicious-tasting, healthy food, good food, happens to be a language we all understand. Fully. *Bien sûr.*

Aggressive problems must be stopped and can be stopped. We're told by many that if we can't help them, they are getting rid of the dog. Nobody wants a vicious, biting dog around the house.

There is no nice way to stop this problem either. If you make excuses that your dog was cruelly treated and that was what made him this way, fine. Even if this is true, you still have to stop the problem. A dog doesn't necessarily have to be treated roughly or cruelly to become mean or vicious. As far as we're concerned, it is not a genetic imprint either. It is a behavioral imprint. The dog learned to be successful by biting and by being vicious. You could have brought up your dog with the best of love and intentions and still have a dog that bites.

Biting dogs are a major problem. The only way to stop this problem is to tackle it head-on. Kisses, kid gloves, and understanding will not work here, at least not at first bite. This problem has to be broken directly, and once you teach the dog that you can do something, too, then you have a chance to use kisses, understanding, and kid gloves later. Rewarding and begging your dog to behave are like putting the cart before the horse. You must make him do what you want him to do first, and then you spoil him rotten.

If you use an electric-shock collar to stop a dog from biting, you will have problems, because when the bite happens, you won't always have the collars on. And if you try to use a choke collar to choke hang your dog every time he bites, the only thing your dog will learn is that the next time you try to put a collar on him, he will bite you before you can get it on him. Why should he let you choke him? And that is what he will think you're going to do, every time you try to put a collar on him.

The way we've found to be the most effective in these extreme cases is our Magic Touch throwing technique, used first full force, and then you can throw a cotton ball and it will work. But don't start off with a cotton ball, use something substantial.

Your dog has to understand that you have something effective and more than a match for his teeth. Throwing also keeps you out of harm's way. Worry less about how it looks if you have to be firm. Care more about the dog living out a long, happy, healthy life. Remember, nothing gets solved with "sit, stay, no," nor is a choke collar, or any other restraining contraption, more humane than a good throw. And a good kiss really works best after your dog has been taught to listen to you.

It was a hot summer's day, the day we had met Melissa, her Red Knight, and Morgan the spellbinding eye gazer. We walked home through Central Park that eve. The Delacorte Theater was presenting Thornton Wilder's *The Skin of Our Teeth*.

Victor—He Bites the Hand That Feeds Him

Lester T. was stressed-out and distraught. He was living in terror and hadn't slept for months. Even in the relative safety of this crowded New Jersey diner, he kept casting furtive glances in every direction, including under the table. He wore a black

Borsalino hat pulled down to meet his thick-rimmed, dark sun-glasses, an overcoat, heavy, knee-high mountain boots, and a pair of thick welder's gloves.

He was trying to make himself as small and as inconspicuous as he possibly could, even smaller than his five-foot-three-inch spindly frame would allow. But how can you be inconspicuous wearing all of these things, including those welder's gloves, in the middle of a hot summer's day? Let alone sporting this out-fit in a restaurant full of people.

It was an effort for him to talk. He was struggling as he slowly unfolded the details of his nightmarish story. This worn-out, weak, and wounded person turned out to be not only emotion-ally scarred, but physically scarred as well.

He made a tentative gesture, nervously pushing his glasses farther up on the bridge of his nose. His face was ghastly. This man had seen things one shouldn't have to see and had expe-rienced things one shouldn't have to experience.

Being eaten alive is not a pleasant experience. But to be eaten alive by a friend, one that you trust, one that you have brought home to live with you as your companion, this is abominable.

This leftover remnant of a man, who used to be Lester T. Thornberry himself, looked like he must've been dragged up-river, seen the very heart of darkness, and never fully recovered.

Lester T. slowly and deliberately removed his thick welder's gloves. Then he rolled up his sleeves, held out his arms, with palms up in a beseeching gesture, and presented them to us for inspection. His left eye rose above the rim of his glasses, and it peered at us as he waited breathlessly for our reaction. But be-fore we could react or say anything, Lester T. moved again.

His arms were still held out in front of him, but now he raised them slightly higher and they hovered above the table for what seemed like an eternity. Then he quickly flipped the palms of his hands over and pushed them toward us. Clearly Lester T. was signaling us: "Wait, don't say a word, be quiet, you haven't seen anything yet. There is much more to come!"

He leaned over, unzipped his boots, pulled them down, and rolled up the legs of his trousers, which revealed a pair of skinny, pipe-cleaner legs. We were flabbergasted at the sight and condition of the limbs of Lester T.

What had happened to him? Could he have been down to South America, gone swimming in the Amazon River or something? Lester T. looked as if he had been chewed up by piranha, as if these little cannibal fish had had him as a blue plate special! And if not cannibals, what was it that was eating Lester T. Thornberry?

Now Lester T. just laid his head down on the table and cried. Poor guy, he was crying his heart out. His glasses schmushed into his face and his black Borsalino fell silently to the floor and lay there forgotten. As soon as he was able to catch his breath, Lester T. began his sorry saga, his tale of woe:

"Can you help me? You must help me, please, please! Victor, my vizsla, has turned into a vindictive, vicious little bastard. I am going to get rid of the rotten son of a bitch. I would have done it already, but my wife, she threatened to leave me if I did. At this point, I don't care if she leaves me, I don't care if everybody leaves me, because if I don't get rid of Victor, he's going to kill me. He's going to finish me off. I can see it now, me lying on the floor and Victor with his teeth clamped around my throat. Just before my eyes close forever, the last thing I see is his wagging, stubby tail. Then, I'm dead. He always wags his tail after biting the hell out of me. Maybe my wife wants it this way, so she can collect the insurance, get the house and everything. Nah, I'm just overreacting a bit. Excuse me a sec, I gotta take my antibiotics and some Valium."

After taking his medication and a stiff drink (mixing tranquilizers with alcohol was against his doctor's orders, but Lester T. did it anyway because he said it made him calmer, faster), Lester T. settled back against the ripped plastic cover of the banquette in our booth. Now, visibly more relaxed and energized, he even managed a faint smile. We think it was a smile, unless he was just a mouther making faces at us. He did look a little green around the gills, but his color and his face-making could have been caused by the combination of his Scotch and medication, mixing with his extralarge wad of chlorophyll chewing gum.

"Victor wasn't always like this. When I first saw the little guy, when I first picked him up and held him in my arms, it was wonderful how he molded like putty in them. I chose him because he was the quietest, shiest, smallest, saddest-looking redhead in this entire family of beautiful Hungarians.

"When I brought him home, he was so shy, so hesitant, that he had to be coaxed to do everything. This may sound wishy-washy to you all, but I felt for the first time in my life someone or something really loved me, for me and me alone. I mean, my wife loves me, sure, but it's a different kind of a love.

"But after a few weeks, little Victor started growling and nipping and becoming very possessive of things. It was soooo cuuuute. So rewarding to watch him grow and gain confidence in himself.

"At first we shook a firm finger at him and told him, 'No.' We stopped doing that when he bit my finger. We shook cans of pennies and quarters at him. We imitated a trainer, I think he was somebody's uncle. He was doing this on TV, this only worked for a day. But Victor became even more and more obstinate. He jumped me and bit me on the wrist that time. I guess he figured the metal soda can would hurt his teeth. Smart puppy.

"We had also purchased a crate to keep our little Victor in

and to train him. It looked horrible, it looked like a small box. I couldn't get him to go in it. He bit me when I tried. I guess it was my fault for trying to put him in a small thing like that. My wife finally got him into the box; he didn't try to bite her, I wonder why?

"Putting Victor in that solitary-confinement box looked so bad, and Victor looking sadly out at us through those bars made us feel like hell.

"We needed a drink, had to have a drink, because it looked so terrible and we felt so guilty.

"As the weeks went by, we drank more and more; it was getting to be a habit with us. First we put him away in his little box, then we drank. All this time, our Victor kept up with us, only his type of nipping was drawing blood; our type of nipping only drew bloodshot eyes. We didn't like it, but we were told by this TV trainer that crates are like 'condos' and dogs simply love to live in them.

"As Victor got older, he got badder. He would go into his crate when he felt like it or when he was angry. One time when he was playing, he hurt his leg; he screamed and ran into the crate. When I tried to get him to come out and reached in to get him, he really tore into me. He put twelve holes into my arms that time. See." Lester T. showed us the holes.

"He generally would go in there with something of ours, something that we didn't want him to have. For example, he took my wallet, my Rolex, even my cell phone, into his condo. We learned through trial, error, and many bites that he only went in there because there was one entrance in and he could protect that entrance with his forty-two beautiful teeth, including four canines, assorted molars, and other types of teeth.

"We had a very nice person come to the house to help us train Victor, but he scared the person away. Victor got worse, he was totally out of control, so we sent him away to be trained and to stop his terrible biting habits.

"He went to a doggy military-type training camp for six months. When he came back, he was like a doggy marine. Before he went away to camp he had been only a talented amateur; now, he had learned to be a professional toothy terrorist.

"His skills in guerrilla warfare had always been natural to begin with. He had been bred to hunt after all, but now his skills had been honed to perfection. He learned surprise sneak attacks. Waiting in ambush, Victor would sometimes lie motionless feigning sleep and then stalk and pounce.

"He would hide in his crate condo or under the couch or under the bed. When he saw me passing by, he would quickly dart out, get two or three fast bites in, and then just as quickly go back to his hideout, one of his caves of security.

"Once he hid in a wall unit that housed the stereo and television and leaped out on me, hitting me square in the chest. Getting up there was a feat only Houdini could duplicate. Once he hid in the back of the closet and surprised me there, when I was reaching in for my boots. I wound up as you see me now with all these new holes in my arms.

"As you can see, I had to start wearing this special equipment just to get near him. It was suggested that I wear this protective gear by both trainers—the love, praise, reward, treat trainer and the tough-guy, discipline-type trainer.

"Maybe I should also have been camouflaged, so he couldn't see me, because he ripped through the coat and the gloves to get at me, he did. He tore me up. I never take off my protective gear now because I never feel secure without it. No matter where I go, I feel Victor breathing down my neck, even if he is not there.

"I just can't relax. So much for love, and so much for the

doggy boot camp. Victor bites like a mean marine, eats like a marine, and drills like a marine. This guy could have been in the Special Forces, a Green Beret at the very least. He's lean and mean, our Victor, the marine.

"But he never bites my wife. Amazing, he loves her. He loves me, too, except he also loves to bite me. Biting me seems to please him more than any other game. If he plays with his toys and I try to join him in his game, he drops the toy he's playing with or stops the game he's playing and tears into me, wagging his tail all the while. After dinner he bites me, instead of lighting up a good cigar.

"I know he loves me. I mean, he sleeps on my side of the bed whenever I'm not home. When I am home, he jumps into bed before me, growls at me, and would bite and chase me if I tried to get into my own bed. I guess I don't really need that bed. He can have it. I do miss my wife, though. I sleep on the couch now.

"But sometimes, if he gets the notion, he'll jump off the bed and go for me on the couch, sending me running for my life, out of the house altogether. Those nights are really bad ones. I have to sleep in the car. Thank God, he doesn't know where the spare keys are or how to open the door to the garage.

"It's tough to argue with such a cute, lovely Hungarian vizsla puppy. I love him, but if you can't help me, now, today, this Sunday, tomorrow, on Monday, he's being killed. I would do it now, on Sunday, but it's a holiday and all the vets are away.

"By the way, I spent all my money on schools and camps and training and vets, and I even lost my business thanks to Victor. I could never work because I'm always hurting and bitten up. So I can't pay you. Why does he only bite me? What did I ever do to him? Except give him the world, a beautiful home in the suburbs on ten acres, three nice cars, cellular phones, the works. He has everything any dog could ever want. If you can't help me, he's a dead dog."

Lester T., by wearing all of that protective clothing, was asking for it. Actually, in Victor's eyes, Lester T. looked threatening, causing Victor to be agitated and frightened and to fight off the agitator in self-defense.

Wearing special gear for protection and slowly approaching a dog in a menacing and agitating way is usually part of a program in the training of attack dogs. Lester T.'s first trainer, the love, praise, and reward one, had told Lester that by wearing something to prevent himself from being bitten, he might be able to get close enough to Victor to praise him, give him a treat or even a kiss, and show Victor what a nice guy he was.

But this dubious piece of advice had had the opposite effect. The more things Lester put on, the more he scared Victor. The more scared Victor got, the more aggressive and unpredictable he would be. And the more aggressive Victor would be, the more frightened and apprehensive Lester would get.

Starting with a little bad advice, everything had gone downhill from there, until Victor became a terrible biter and Lester became terribly frightened of his dog. The nice trainer, following his own advice, had tried to give Victor a kiss, but had been rewarded with a painful bite on the nose. He quit.

Because of Lester's tale of terror, we entered his house with a great deal of caution. We were prepared for some kind of confrontation. We know that if the dog decides to establish himself aggressively, we need to be ready to respond in kind. Of course we had heard only one side of the story, Lester T.'s.

We were pleasantly surprised, however. When we walked in, Victor didn't challenge us in any way, he wasn't aggressive. We did what any invited guest would do, we walked in and sat down.

Victor seemed happy to see us. He was a sweetheart, a

friendly guy. He didn't try to bite us, he was just a frisky, rambunctious two-year-old. There is no need to become aggressive if the dog isn't. But we were still prepared, just in case Victor was merely taking his time and sizing us up for a good bite.

When we felt certain that Victor wasn't going to challenge us, we started right into our Magic Touch program. Victor had to learn to trust and listen to his owners from now on. This was his last chance.

Because Lester T. was living in such fear of his dog, we first worked with his wife, Sharon. She was great. In about ten minutes flat she had Victor eating out of the palm of her hand. He was coming to her and following her around the house. Sharon was actually a strong person with her dog, she just needed a way to go with him, some right information, and a few adjustments. We put that into her hands, literally, with our Magic Touch. We get people like Sharon from time to time who get the hang of our philosophy immediately, and it didn't hurt that she had the accuracy of a major league pitcher.

Sharon's main headache was when the doorbell rang or when there was an outside noise. Immediately, Victor, barking insanely, would start off on his mad routine, first running to the door and then to the windows. Building up speed, he would run wildly around the house, running so fast that the centrifugal force would actually lift him off the floor and onto the walls as if he were defying gravity.

The window shades were torn to shreds by this dog running across them. Could something be done to stop this destruction? We immediately saw what she meant when a noise set him off. His running around the walls was quite funny. It reminded us of a Fred Astaire movie where Fred would dance on the walls and then go dancing across the ceiling. Although it did seem funny at the time, it was quite destructive.

Sharon stopped Victor quite simply with three accurate

throws of a magazine. She caught him in flight and he stopped. Remember, when you throw something and your dog stops what he's doing, you always tell him how good he is for listening to you.

This wouldn't have worked so quickly if we hadn't first taught Victor to go to Sharon. Her Victor was so perfect so fast that it made our job easy. Jokingly we suggested to Sharon that the best thing for her to do was to get rid of one Lester T. Thornberry. Lester T. didn't think it was so funny.

Now Lester T. Thornberry, seeing for the first time a way to stay out of harm's way and yet still get his dog to listen to him, wanted to try. It was time to test the mettle and take the measure of the man. We had to get Lester T. to trust us enough to take off his outlandish outfit. It was also time to take off the gloves. The gloves would now be his gauntlet to throw. Would Victor be the victor in this contest of wills? Or would it be Lester T.?

Our Lester T. didn't throw immediately, he was tentative. Was he insecure? Was he nervous? Or was he just readying himself, warming up? We'll never know the answer. But we do know it took Lester T. a full twenty minutes of preparation, of warning his dog, of shaking his gloves back and forth at his dog.

Finally, with a little prodding from Sharon, and by placing himself safely behind a large chair, he finally, finally threw his gloves at Victor—missing him by a mile.

Victor, confused and puzzled by Lester T.'s bizarre ballet, ignored him, walked over to Sharon, and leaned against her for moral support. Now Lester T.'s ire was up, way up. Boy, was he pissed off. It seemed Lester T. could endure anything from his dog, and he did, but to have his dog totally ignore him in the company of strangers was the last straw, the final insult.

He stepped out from behind the chair, he picked up a magazine (a small one—certain habits are hard to give up), he threw it at Victor. It hit him (just barely). Victor looked up at Sharon with a long-suffering look in his eyes and then walked slowly right over to Lester T. The mettle of the man had been halfway proven and was to be tested further. But half is better than none.

The boudoir was where Lester and Sharon had the most problems, with Victor we mean. His toys were all over the floor and he refused to allow anyone near them. He wouldn't get off the bed either. He would plant himself on Lester T.'s side and not move. In these situations he became quite obstinate and nasty, snarling and snapping if anyone came near him. Now we saw Victor the bad, living up to his bad reputation.

Many times dogs, as they grow from puppyhood on up, want to possess small things, small personal things such as toys, shoes, and socks. As they grow older, they want more—the bed-room, the living room, every room. Soon they want to possess the whole house, and anybody in the house or coming into the house.

As the dog gets older, he might still not be satisfied and need even more—the city, the state, the country, everything be-comes his possession. This dog, if not stopped, might want to rule the world, becoming king of the world, like the director of the movie *Titanic*. So, before this happens to you, we think, when a puppy shows any nasty aggression, he should be stopped before he orders you out of his world.

Lester T., now feeling his oats, threw a paperback book at Victor and Victor got off the bed. Lester threw again to get Victor to drop and walk away from his possessions on the floor. This also worked. Now, for the first time, Lester T. was able to pick something up off the floor and not get bitten.

The dangerous closet hiding place was neutralized immedi-ately by throwing. Now when Lester T. called Victor out of the closet, he came over and sat down next to him. Lester T. told him how good he was and scratched Victor's head affectionately. All other problem places that Victor pounced from were neutralized in the same way.

Lester T. Thornberry was finally able to look at himself in the mirror and actually smile. He seemed to like the magic that was really only common sense.

If your dog aggressively guards something that you don't want him to have, and you feel that you might get bitten if you reach down to take it away from him, don't reach down. Trust your instincts, you're probably right. Don't put yourself in harm's way.

Instead, try throwing something. This will help your dog change his mind about biting you, and it will make him walk away from the object of contention. If he doesn't walk away, throw again until he does. When he moves away, praise him. When you throw, throw something relatively substantial.

Let the size of the dog determine the size of the object. A cotton ball does not an impression make when tossed at a Great Dane, a Doberman, or for that matter, even at a Maltese. If what you throw is not substantial enough, you could get bitten. The next time, you'll know to use something that makes more of an impression.

The first time we're challenged, we like to use more not less. We know a sneaker works. Don't use a shoe with high heels or hard soles, which could be dangerous to the dog. We know a magazine works. Don't use a hardcover book, that could be dangerous to your dog.

Never corner your dog. If he is in a corner, move to one side. Stand back and throw and let him have the option of leaving. It is important that your dog know he can back down or go away at any time. Give him a way out. Always.

Never put yourself in harm's way. If your dog confronts you, your throwing will keep you out of harm's way and will control the action. Remember, don't miss, don't warn him, don't corner him, and don't stop until he backs down. If it's a draw, you lose. Don't practice this; you should only get into this confrontation if your dog doesn't give you any other choice.

Lester T. Thornberry got a new leash on life. Victor got a permanent stay of execution. Sharon was out looking for a contract to pitch for the New York Yankees. We got lunch. It was barbecued chicken and garlic mashed potatoes.

We were joined by a happy and well-adjusted, four-legged, hungry Hungarian, Victor. We learned that Lester T.'s middle name was Timothy. Tim for short, and just plain old Mr. T. for shorter.

CHAPTER 13

Breaking the Codes

Beyond Physical Evidence

Investigations involve concentrated and detailed observations. What can be wrong is not necessarily what you see. The story we get when we arrive on a case is one thing, and this drama can be rather interesting. What the dog or cat tells us could be quite another bunch of facts. Different facts, to be sure, but still interesting.

As a case develops, a more complete picture starts to take shape. New dimensions are revealed. Events start to take on a life of their own.

Physical evidence is collected, listed, and bagged. Some can go to the lab for further detailed analysis. Pertinent information is jotted down to be later checked and rechecked. You never know where the answers will come from.

It used to be that a tip could come from a stoolie dropping a thin dime, but now the phone companies have raised their rates. Information doesn't come cheap anymore, it could cost you plenty to get what you need.

But what you're seeing here, what will have been collected up to now, are just the clues of the physical evidence, bits and pieces from a collection of questionable data.

Snap judgments formed from this scattered collection of incomplete or pseudo evidence could lead to bad judgments. The fickle finger of fate may be shaken at an innocent victim, who could end up facing and suffering dire consequences.

This could result in irreversible damages, damages that may never be remedied in any court in the world, civil or criminal. It might mean the end of an innocent. Another Billy Budd hits the deck.

Being preoccupied with the physical evidence alone, you could miss solving the case altogether.

The whys are missing, the much needed psychological answers. They are to be found elsewhere. They are to be found only in the minds of the players. The whys definitely go to motive.

These mind factors, the psychological, emotional, and metaphysical sides of a case, are not found under your nose, they are not thrown in front of you, these clams don't open up so fast, don't give up their secrets so easily. They have to be ferreted out, mined, dug up, dragged to the surface, sometimes kicking and screaming and sometimes delicately lifted. The dimensions of the mind are not so easy to see or to get at.

Put all the elements together. Look at the whole picture, get the complete story. Sift through the sand, dig up the dirt, look at the prints left behind by the parties in question. Always keeping in mind never to disturb any of the evidence. Prints are fleeting and fragile. We must get to them fast, before they are covered by the incoming tide, washed away by cleaning fluid, or sucked up by a vacuum.

When we're called in on a case and we're looking for a way to go, we need all the clues. Not just the physical clues, but all the clues. No leads are too small to look at, no stone will be left unturned.

But what sticks in our craw are the red herrings. Sometimes you step in 'em, sometimes you trip over 'em. Sometimes the herrings send you off in the wrong direction entirely. Sometimes they stink, sometimes you have them with cream sauce, and sometimes you have them with wine sauce. Later on, you might find some of that sauce on your shirt.

But these cases are not about fish, although some sure smelled fishy at the time. Some were elementary and some were quite puzzling. But all were quite stimulating to say the least.

Fear of Animals

The Inheritance

Everyone at the petting zoo was having a great time, especially all the animals. They were getting praised, petted, and pampered. Capricorn, a baby goat, approached four-year-old Jenny. She wanted something to eat. Nervously, Jenny stared at the little goat. The little goat stared expectantly at the bag of nuts and fruit Jenny held clenched in her fist.

Teri, Jenny's mother, pleased that this small, lovely creature had taken an interest in her daughter, decided to step out of the way and give Jenny a chance to get to know the little goat better and maybe strike up a friendship.

This was a first step in a grand plan that Teri was trying to hatch. A plan to put an end to her daughter's fear of animals. The little goat would be a perfect start, and a great help.

Jenny was so focused on the little goat, she didn't notice her mom backing away. The goat never hesitated, not for an instant, but came right up to her and tried to grab the bag of food out of Jenny's hand. Jenny jerked her hand back and screamed for her mother's help.

She closed her eyes tightly and stamped her feet wildly in a frantic maneuver, hoping the goat would disappear. But she didn't disappear. The temptation of the nuts and fruit was too overpowering.

Even while facing the threat of imminent danger, the possibility of being attacked and swallowed whole by a friendly, little baby goat, with a tiny mouth, Jenny still didn't let go of her bag of nuts and fruit. Her hand clung to the bag as if it were glued there.

The little goat, surprised at such resistance, stuck her tongue out and made a high-pitched bleating sound of her own, then came even closer and grabbed the bag.

Jenny freaked. The girl and the goat were now securely attached by a plastic bag of nuts and fruit, and neither would give it up. Jenny because she was too frozen in fear to let go of her end, and the goat because she was determined to get that bag of tasty goodies. Fear and opportunity faced each other, attached securely by a simple, nonbiodegradable plastic baggy.

Jenny, thinking that her mother was right there, right next to her and ready to help in an instant, reached for Mom with her free hand. But to her not so happy surprise, Mom wasn't there, Mom wasn't where she was supposed to be.

Jenny quickly opened her eyes to see where Mom was, and when she spotted her target of salvation, Jenny dove over and grabbed Teri's leg, holding on to it for dear life, screaming and crying. But even while diving, screaming, and crying, she still hung on to the bag of nuts and fruit, which was still being held on to by Capricorn, the little goat.

These were not the bonding connections and friendships Teri had hoped for when she had brought her daughter to the petting zoo to see and play with all the animals. Now a three-way security attachment was in place. The goat, the daughter, and the mom all held together by a soft but durable plastic bond.

Two zookeepers came running over and broke off the plastic binding bond. They separated the goat from the bonding attachment, but left the mother and daughter's attachment still in place. The keepers wanted to know what was wrong. Had the little goat done something wrong, or had the little girl hurt herself in some way, and could they be of any help?

Capricorn looked confused. Nobody was paying any attention to her or giving her any food. She would have enjoyed both. Even with all of this confusion going on, Teri caught the goat's eye and understood immediately. Both kids were upset.

With her grand plan now in shambles and feeling guilty for completely screwing everything up, Teri took her crying, screaming daughter out of the zoo and tossed the whole bag of nuts and fruit over to little Capricorn, who perked up when the goodies arrived airmail.

Little Capricorn was probably not affected by this incident, except to learn that not every child is friendly and outgoing. What did Jenny learn, if anything? And what about Teri, who had set up this shambled play date?

Had Jenny been able to relax, these two kids might have found a common bond. The goat had come over in friendship and for just a little something to eat. She knew nothing of fear, she wasn't frightened of Jenny. But Jenny hadn't taken the goat's interest as a friendly gesture. She had been too frightened to take up the offer of a friendly get-together.

Fear, a horse of a different color, had also entered the petting zoo and stood, a barrier to friendship between Jenny and Capricorn.

What had made Jenny so frightened of this small, friendly creature? Most young animals, including human animals, have an innate curiosity about each other and aren't usually terrified when introduced, unless something has made them that way. Somewhere along the line, a behavioral imprint of fear had been instilled in Jenny.

Capricorn, like all babies who have had only positive experiences, had been direct in her actions. When she saw something good, such as food, and she wanted it, she went after it. She didn't think about whether it was okay or risky or if it was the right thing to do socially. In her environment, a protected zoo society, she had no notions of danger.

Perhaps when she grows older, Capricorn might have more problems with social acceptance. Horns, size, and speed, for sure, in her case, will change things. Beauty is in the eye of the beholder, and everybody loves babies.

As far as Jenny was concerned, she was also growing up in a protected environment. So why was she, at this early age, so loaded with anxiety and fear?

The incident at the zoo had been the catalyst. The decision was made that "something had to be done." Teri couldn't understand why her four-year-old daughter, Jenny, was so frightened of animals. She had never been attacked, bitten, or hurt in any way by any animals, including dogs or cats.

This irrational fear was bothering Teri quite a bit; she felt responsible for her daughter's fear of animals. The end results were always the same, panic and fright.

Whenever Jenny saw a dog or a cat, or even on visits to the zoo if any animals showed any interest in her, she would immediately react by grabbing for her mother, locking herself onto Mom's legs and holding on for dear life.

We took a walk in Central Park with Teri. At first, this well-spoken and confident person impressed us. She would look you right in the eye and say whatever was on her mind. She appeared to be direct, at ease, and strong. But all of this changed quickly when any dogs came around her. It was as if she had two completely different personalities.

Plenty of dogs were around on this sunny Saturday afternoon. Teri's reactions to all the dogs were clear enough. She felt uncomfortable when any of them came near her.

Her smooth, rhythmic way of speaking would immediately change. Her sentences would break up, she would hesitate over her choice of words, and her voice went up higher. Her attention was distracted from us and became focused on the dogs who happened close by. She fixed her stares and directed her conversation and attention to them.

If anyone was benefiting from her talk, it was clearly the dogs. Teri might ostensibly have been talking to us, but she was definitely looking at them. Her formerly impressive eye contact was gone, nowhere to be seen.

The dogs collected her attention and her talk and left well informed. We had to grab at her words as they passed us on the way to the dogs. When someone is intensely talking to you, but staring in another direction, it is difficult to grasp what they are saying.

Some of the dogs were nice, knew she was scared, and so didn't press her for attention. Other dogs knew she was scared and couldn't resist giving her a little razzmatazz, a little bit of doggy dos and don'ts: a couple of jumps, plenty of drool, some happy whining, and some heavy barking. These dogs enjoyed pushing her around; in her frightened state, she became their game ball.

Still other dogs didn't care too much for her high-voiced conversation. It hurt their eardrums and delicate sensibilities. They went on their way without further comment. Going for a swim, a cool dip in the boat lake, they couldn't be bothered with this person who had such a negative reaction to their good looks.

This person was clearly frightened of dogs and any other animals that would get close to her, including the fabulous Central Park squirrels, pigeons, ducks, and all other harmless free souls. Why?

Here she was on the one hand saying she couldn't understand why her daughter was so afraid of animals, that there wasn't any cause for it, and on the other hand, she was showing us plenty of cause for her daughter to be afraid.

The main cause was the role model herself, Mom. Mom was saying one thing, but acting out in an entirely different manner, losing her composure every time a dog got close to her or passed by.

The answer was right there, right in front of her nose. Teri was playing out the same scenario as her daughter, except that, being an adult, she could cover her fears a little better, with a more sophisticated set of defenses.

When we pointed this out to her, she admitted being frightened of dogs and cats ever since she was a child, even though she had never been bitten or threatened by any herself.

It turned out that Teri's mother had once been bitten by a dog, or at least her mother had said this had happened. But this wasn't known for sure. Teri never really knew if her mother had ever been bitten or not.

As she was growing up, her mother had always pulled her away from dogs. Her mother had continually said things like

"Doesn't that dog look vicious, mean, and dirty?" The thoughts had been firmly planted in Teri. This behavioral imprint was in place, loaded into the system.

As Teri grew up, she grew up frightened of dogs and other animals because of this programming. Without consciously thinking about it, Teri was passing on these fears to her daughter.

Jenny was growing up frightened, and there would be another generation of fearful people in this family, with no foundation for it. This inherited line of fear had to be broken somewhere and by someone, and Teri was going to be it. She was determined to make sure this inheritance of fear would stop with her.

Teri and her therapist had come up with a plan to solve the problem. They had decided that she would never mention anything negative about dogs or other animals to consciously frighten her daughter. They had decided that she would slowly and selectively introduce Jenny to small, friendly, nonthreatening animals, in a safe, controlled environment, such as the petting zoo.

But their plan wasn't working at all. The inherited fear wasn't going away. Teri couldn't understand why their ideas weren't having the positive effects she had hoped for.

Talking and rationalizing can help you understand a problem, but they are limited in scope and don't go far enough. Confronting the problem head-on, in its actual state, that's where it has to be met and neutralized.

Just to bring a child, who has this fear, around animals will not teach that child not to fear them. Animals react, too. You have to know about animals in order to work this problem out.

We explained to Teri that even though she wasn't consciously telling her daughter to be frightened of dogs and cats, she was showing her fear in many other more telling ways.

All of Teri's psychological fears were showing up in instinctive physical actions. Tensing up, squeezing her daughter's hand without thinking, stepping back when a dog got too close, pushing or pulling Jenny behind her whenever she saw a dog, voice and language changes, all of these signs Jenny was picking up as fear and weakness.

There was no question about it, the tension showed. Unconsciously, without intending to do so, Teri was instilling this fear into the young, impressionable mind of her child. Unconsciously, Teri was being her own mother.

We choreographed a set of moves so that, even though Teri was frightened, she wouldn't look frightened or sound frightened to her daughter.

When you are frightened of dogs or cats, consciously or unconsciously you send out messages, signals. Animals can read these codes with ease. They will pick up the signs and act accordingly; each will react according to his own personality.

Scramble the code. Make it hard for them to read and break down. Learn to disguise the message. Create a new modus operandi.

We explained to Teri, when you are frightened or angry, your adrenaline starts pumping. The smells of fright and anger register the same to dogs and cats. You can't disguise them. Dogs and cats are also the experts on body language. So, to fool the experts, you have to cleverly disguise your body language to hide your true feelings.

When afraid, you would instinctively want to move backward. Instead, you have to do the opposite and move forward. Your hand movements, instead of being defensive, now have to become aggressive and express confidence.

And most of all, either be quiet, say nothing, or lower your voice and give it some strength. A high, squeaky voice, with no air behind it, means what it sounds like. It is a dead giveaway of fright.

We felt as if we were choreographing a Broadway show with Teri. Only these acts were for real. The stakes were higher here: a generational fear line had to be broken and rebuilt. Moves were worked out for Teri to learn and to practice. We rehearsed them with her until she got the idea.

It's a fifty-fifty proposition. Sometimes we teach behavioral direction and redirection to our animals, and sometimes we have to do the same with people. It's a toss-up on who gets it right and how long it takes.

When a dog is coming over to you, friendly or not, take a couple of good deep breaths, get some oxygen in those lungs, say something strong, cheer yourself on, and take a couple of sure steps forward. Now, stop walking, and you'll notice that the dog is either slowing down or stopping, too. You are now not such an easy mark in his eyes. He'll want to think about taking you on now, since you didn't back away when he approached you.

We also showed Teri that if she tossed something, the animal would stop or go away altogether. We didn't want her to use the Magic Touch unless it was really necessary, if a dog was aggressive toward her. But Teri had to learn the technique anyway. It gave her an extra boost of confidence. She now had her very own Dumbo's feather.

It took a couple of walks with Teri to change and then reinforce her moves. As she started to face her fears, she was able to relax more around dogs. When we went out with Teri and Jenny, the new moves started working.

Teri eventually got her daughter to accept dogs and cats. But this would probably always be a struggle for Teri herself.

It's like learning to ride a horse. If you grow up around horses and you learn to ride them as a child, then the riding becomes natural, a natural extension of your relationship with your horse. If you learn how to ride as an adult, even though you can become a good rider, it still is work and practice.

Teri, seeing the success of her efforts, her daughter being happily around and accepting animals, enjoyed her accomplishment. Teri continued on her program—sometimes nervously laughing, stepping forward, being uncomfortable at times, but always doing her best to hide her nervousness for the sake of her daughter. Letting go of her daughter's hand around dogs was Teri's last give up of fear. But she did it.

She always kept in mind, and she made sure Jenny knew, that you should never walk up to a dog and touch him without asking permission of the owner.

This is not only the right thing to do, but it's also safe.

Emotional fears, even with minimal foundations in a physical reality, can still affect many and have a powerful psychological reach. Imaginary fears, fears of the unknown, can be overwhelming.

Some people who have seen scary events dramatized, such as a shark attack in the movie *Jaws*, never swim in the ocean again. Ever. Seeing a plane crash, some people will never want to fly again. Ever.

But for the daring, and for those who want their children not to be afraid of dogs and cats, fake it. Take a deep breath, laugh, and step forward. Let your children know that all dogs, cats, and other animals are not so bad, even if they've seen *Cujo*.

Fending Off the Wild Biters

An inherited fear of animals, based on hearsay events, is quite different from a fear caused by an actual incident. A person who has been bitten for real knows how much it hurts. The biting incident has lasting effects, effects you don't forget so quickly or so easily.

Once you've been bitten, you might become frightened and uncomfortable around animals and want to stay away from them for good. Or, you can chalk up the bite as an isolated incident, understand that although animals can bite, not all are ready to bite you, and know that you are not going to get bitten every time you come into contact with one.

If you fall off a horse and you get back on, then the fall becomes part of your riding experience and you are not afraid. You're not left with any residual fear of horses. You just know that you could fall off. Big deal. Falling sometimes goes with the territory.

If you let the fall be the bigger part of your experience with horses and you don't get back on, if you come to believe that every time you get on a horse you're going to fall off, then you don't ride anymore. You become frightened of riding and possibly of horses altogether—even though your bad experience might have occurred through no fault of your own and might have been just a fluke accident.

The same transference of fear can be seen in cases involving dogs, cats, or other animals. A bad experience can leave you frightened for life, or you can let the experience teach you an awareness that can be helpful to you in the future. With your newfound experience, hard won, you might avoid trouble the next time. We learn from our experiences and mistakes.

There are lessons that can help you deal with uncomfortable or dangerous situations. Information that you can use, whether you have been bitten or not, whether you are afraid or not. If you are threatened by an animal, knowing what to do can help you get out of a bad or seemingly impossible situation.

The more you know about your situation the better you can handle it. Knowledge can help neutralize and overcome many fears. Fears that are based on the unknown. What is the animal going to do, and what are you going to do?

Screaming and yelling rarely works and could even make an animal wilder and more aggressive.

Aggressive body posturing is helpful. But you are limited to your acting abilities and looks alone.

If you push, grab, or kick out at a dog, cat, or other fast-moving animal, know that he is faster than you, and by taking these actions you have a good chance of getting bitten or worse.

By doing these things, you're showing the animal all that you can do, your limitations, the extent of your physical abilities. You have no more weapons left in your arsenal to show. If it's enough, you win. If it isn't enough, you lose. In the case of a large animal, you not only lose, but you could lose an awful lot.

Instinctively, the first thing people want to do when they see a dog or larger animal coming after them aggressively is to turn and run. But running isn't a good option when trying to outrun the fleet of foot. In this contest, they'll beat you every time.

You do have one really good ally though, the throwing technique. Throwing is an excellent way to protect yourself. It gives you a dimension that the animal has trouble getting around or understanding. Knowing the Magic Touch technique is powerful knowledge to have under your belt. Even if you don't have an animal of your own, never want one, or never want to see one. Life has a way of throwing the unexpected at you; now you can have the ability to throw something back.

If confronted, throw. Throw hard, throw fast, and keep throwing until the aggressor breaks off his attack. Don't back up unless you have to. Step forward instead. Always keep facing the aggressive animal. If he goes to one side, you turn and face him. If he tries to get behind you, turn around and face him.

As for the usual, dubious advice, to stand totally still and make believe you are a tree or to lie down and act like a log, this advice only works for trees and logs. Trees and logs are used as territorial markers for animals and are homes for ants and termites.

If you Method act in this manner, there's a good chance you might get bitten or peed on, or both, because urinating is a form of aggression, too, it's another way dogs, cats, or other animals will mark off their territory. Don't forget, while you're lying there being a tree, the ants might decide to move in and get to know you better. Ants bite.

When hiking or camping, if you are aggressively confronted and threatened by a bear or a mountain lion, your best shot is to throw and keep throwing.

Pick up anything you can find, rocks, sticks, anything substantial, and throw. The throwing is something these animals do not understand, and once you unleash your supersense, and as strongly as you can, you have a better than good chance of making them go away. Remember, you are probably looked at as a food source. So don't be food for their thought, change their mind. Let them go find an easier meal elsewhere.

Also keep in mind, these wild animals live in this domain, you are the intruder. Some might have young to protect, and all parents are very protective. So use your common sense. Try to be a caring visitor when passing through. Only protect yourself by throwing if it becomes truly necessary.

Live and Let Live

In any relationship, nobody is expected to get along all the time, every waking moment. We all have our idiosyncrasies, good and bad points, and testy moments.

Don't force animals into friendships. If you have a cat and a dog in the house and they don't get along, don't try to force them to like each other. But don't let them fight either or, as some say, work out their differences in their own way. You break up any fighting, any confrontations. You manage the safety and well-being of those cats and dogs. If they see you taking care of things and they see they can trust their security with you, they'll settle down.

The same with dogs to dogs. Don't press friendships. Don't let them work things out for themselves either. Working it out could mean a fight. And someone is going to get hurt, usually the smaller and weaker someone. You must make certain that everything stays smooth. You don't want any ripples in your lake.

Don't force people and animals into friendships. If you meet someone and he doesn't like your dog or cat, or he is frightened of your dog or cat, don't force them to get along. Don't play silly games. Respect his wanting to be left alone. Chase your cat or dog away from him if they are bothering your friend. The same goes in reverse.

If a friend is annoying your cat or dog who doesn't want to be bothered, stop the person from being a pain in the ass. Your insensitivity and lack of respect for the feelings of your animals, in this case, could cause them to take the necessary steps on their own to get rid of this annoyance.

Respect each other's space. Live and let live. It works all the time. These are good formulas that work.

In some households some love cats and dogs, some can't stand cats and dogs. Some inherit cats and dogs for one reason or another, usually through a new relationship. To keep the new grouping together, there will have to be some kind of understanding and tolerance.

Stopping aggression is one thing, getting an animal to love

and accept you is another story. It is possible to coexist without liking, loving, or getting along all the time.

Masking a Fear of Animals: Pinky the Pocket Poodle

She worked with violent patients. She was a nonviolent person, this psychiatrist. The apparent paradox of her work and her beliefs didn't seem to bother Dr. Pauline. That a violent confrontation could occur and threaten her safety and well-being didn't seem to enter her mind as a possibility.

She had built a safety net of rationalizations, theories, and conclusions around herself. A net woven tight by psychiatric study, by ands, ifs, and possibles. She referenced a long line of mind-benders, whose work could be shifted and shaped to fit her theories.

She was fortunate that thought could be so pliable, that something, somehow, some way, like a good dress, could always be made to fit. She felt she could change and defuse most violent personalities and bring them back into society as productive, peaceful citizens.

The doctor felt certain of her work, that her "cured" could walk the world again in peace and not pose a danger to anyone, anywhere, at any time. She felt her "cured" were cured for good. Just a little touch-up visit from time to time.

There were inherent problems, however, in her world. An explosion was imminent. But for now, the dynamite lay dormant and sweating, it went unnoticed. The setter off of the fuse, the one who would light it, came from an unexpected quarter. But whether expected or not, he was there. He was in place. Right under her nose, and sometimes on it. A day of reckoning was not far off. A day that would sorely test the doctor's confidence and her commitment to her beliefs.

The nonviolent psychiatrist with her violent caseload confidently went about her business, she was in charge. Even though some of her patients were vicious criminals, even killers who had been locked away to keep society safe, Dr. P. continued to apply peaceful, soft pillows to feather, cushion, and ease the troubled minds. This peaceful person felt that she had total control over all the troubled waters that flooded into her office.

But in troubled waters can sometimes swim unknown fish and red herrings.

If ever one of these violent souls started to twitch, became agitated, hung on the edge of a violent episode to be acted out in the office, peaceful Pauline felt she could still control the situation peacefully and nonviolently. She said all she had to do was push a button. The button technique never failed her.

The button brought brawny Bernard and burly Benjamin. These two button men were Pauline's enormous, not so peaceful assistants.

Bernard and Benjamin, both former professional defensive linemen, could wrestle and put down the most violent of episodes, real fast. The doctor supplied all the professional peacefulness, Bernard and Benjamin supplied all the professional muscle and brawn to keep the peace.

Dr. P. told us that when Bernard and Benjamin played professional football, they would indiscriminately scoop up the other team in total. Cast away the players they didn't want, until they found the hapless ballcarrier, the one they did want.

Bernard and Benjamin had no problem taking down a single, agitated, violent patient and dressing him in a straitjacket. Then, it was an easy task for the peaceful doctor to walk over and solicitously inquire of the patient, "Are you all right? Should we give you something to calm you down?"

Practical Pauline didn't wait for an answer. She wouldn't have been able to hear one anyway, because the patient would be in shock from the tackling and wouldn't have been able to get a word out from under Bernard and Benjamin, who would be sitting on top of him. The twitching patient, buried beneath the combined weight of the button men, would be solely concentrating on trying to breathe.

There is nothing like a nice sedative to calm the nerves down, thought Dr. P. A shot here and some therapy there was just what the doctor ordered.

With all of this control and knowledge going for her, why then was Pinky so violent? Why wouldn't he behave?

Here was the swimming fish, the smelly red herring. The troubled water, the dynamite, the fish that would put her to the test. This fish was Pinky, her violent, out-of-control pocket poodle.

Dr. P. had us fooled at first. She said everything was great, "basically." The few times that Pinky had bit her on the nose were just breakdowns in their communication, they were only accidents. She was certain he hadn't meant to do it. Dr. P. felt as soon as she fully explained to Pinky what he was doing wrong, he would understand and stop. This was just a basic misunderstanding, "basically." It was probably her fault for giving him the wrong signals, but now she felt they had reached a better understanding. She had bought him toys and cookies to celebrate their new togetherness.

Basically. *A cover-up word, heavily recycled. A basic clue that all was not kosher here.*

Bribes. *Aka rewards. Also used as cover-ups and buy-offs. They come in many different shapes and flavors.*

When Dr. P. tried to pick Pinky up, to show us how beautiful and well-behaved he was, she was tentative and hesitant. She couldn't find the right way to take hold of him, he was more than a handful for her.

She finally grabbed him, picked him up, looked at us triumphantly, and Pinky, with a gleam in his eye, turned around and bit her hard. Pinky had "basically" gone into action.

This energetic ball of dynamite clamped tightly onto her nose. "Help me! Get him off my nose!" Pauline cried nasally. The dog looked like a climber fastened to a face on Mount Rushmore. It didn't look good. No one looks good wearing a poodle on the nose. We pried him loose.

The doctor clamped a towel to her nose, to stop the bleeding. "I just wanted to give Pinky a kiss." Pauline found herself in a quandary. All her training, schooling, and experience had not prepared her for this situation. She had never come up against it before. She had never been attacked or hurt by anyone, let alone by a little dog with no violent past.

She pulled down all her research books looking for answers she might have missed. But her mentors and guides failed her. She couldn't find a proper slot for this type of behavior. It wasn't to be found in any weighty volume assessing violent behavior. Pinky's directness threw her for a loop and scared her. His actions were speaking louder than any of her words.

The more she patiently reasoned with Pinky, the more he directly focused on her nose. Each time she lectured him, he patiently sat and listened, his eyes following her every word and expression. From the way he watched her, with such interest and attention, she was convinced that he understood her.

But then, as soon as the lecture ended, it was the trigger for him to take aim, jump up, and get hold of her knowledge and her nose. He was ambidextrous, he could do both at one time, bite her nose and absorb her knowledge.

Pinky's preference for this permanent perch and his perforations of her prominent proboscis left peaceful Pauline perplexed and punctured. Her tides were ebbing and flowing out of control. Band-Aids, counseling, and bribes hadn't helped, not one bit.

"I work with the most violent criminals in my practice and I've never been attacked, let alone by a sociopathic, four-pound poodle with his extreme acting-out fits of violence. I've tried everything that I could think of."

Sociopathic? A clue, but what did it mean, exactly?

Now the apology game started.

"I thought maybe it was because I left Pinky alone too long. But I did apologize to him for that. Perhaps I inadvertently ignored him? I apologized to him for that also. I don't know, I probably did something else wrong, but I apologized to him for that, too. I know that I shouldn't have yelled at him and I did and I also apologized to him for that. I don't know, it seems the more I apologize and try to make up to him, the more violent and aggressive he becomes." The doctor was doing some fast talking, and losing control at warp speed. Valium seemed to be the required prescription for Pauline.

We asked Pauline, now that she was a bit calmer, had she ever given Pinky a good slap for this biting of the nose job? Sometimes a direct action requires an equally direct reaction.

From behind the bloody towel on her nose, Pauline patiently explained to us that she didn't believe in being physical to solve any behavioral problems. "As I've already told you, in my job I don't believe in using any form of physical force, not even with my violent patients. Violence begets violence."

We gave her a simple scenario. If one of her patients had a bat in his hand and was looking to hurt her, how would she deal with it?

Pauline said, "That's easy. My Bernard and Benjamin would grab that person, take away the bat, and render him helpless in seconds, until I can talk some sense into him."

There was the answer for the doctor's problem. Take Bernard and Benjamin home with her and, when Pinky got violent, have them hold him down until she could talk some sense into him. Or, there was the option of a well-placed slap, tit for tat, for the painful biting episodes.

Pauline considered our remedy and discarded it as too violent. Instead, she gave Pinky away. She felt that was a better option for both of them, that this small, macho dog would do better bonding with the guys. She gave him to the only two she considered strong enough to control Pinky's inclinations toward violence, Bernard and Benjamin.

The ex–football players were delighted with their pocket poodle tough guy. Pinky settled down and became a nice guy when he realized that the B & B noses weren't to be used for climbing or hanging on to.

Pauline was actually frightened of her dog but hid this fear behind a professional mask, a mask of fear in its ultimate form, a mask that she called nonviolent. The dog had blown this cover, so he had to go. Pauline could now go back to her successful formulas and her winning ways.

Pinky knew in many ways that Pauline was frightened of him. He knew it by her smell and he knew it by the way she moved and attempted to pick him up. Her movements were ones of fear and uncertainty.

Pinky was an aggressive dog and had to be put in his place. Pauline couldn't do it. Although he was only four pounds, he was too much dog for her. Size is in the heart. And kindness can sometimes be mistaken for weakness. Dr. Pauline was a professionally kind person.

We almost slipped on the red herrings the doctor threw down in front of us. These herrings of confidence, of knowing her dog, her herrings of making excuses for the biting, backing up the excuses with high-sounding, highfalutin terminology and analysis, these were very slippery red herrings indeed.

She had also allowed the vagaries of her professional life to influence her judgments about her little dog. She took the suppressed and barely controlled violent tendencies of her patients and transferred them into Pinky's biting personality. She saw Pinky as one of her violent patients to be analyzed and cured. In Pinky's case, a simple biting problem had been blown out of all proportion.

Summed up in a few little words, the doctor was truly afraid of her dog. No amount of roundabout psychology was going to change that.

When the worlds of the two-legged and the four-legged, the metaphysical and the real, collide, they sometimes explode. Prints identifying the true nature and direction of a case can be covered up by layers of sand and time.

Authentic and important clues necessary to solve a case can be buried. When they are buried in the mind, how long will they be there until seeing the light of day? And what shape will the clues be in when found?

The psychology of fear can be an especially difficult barrier to break down and overcome. Whether real or make-believe, fear can be overwhelming and controlling. The faces of fear show themselves in many different ways. Responses to imaginary or real dangers, lurking in the unknown, are complex.

There are many codes to break when solving a case. Mind games, when expertly played, are quite tricky and sensitive. When feelings and emotions are at stake, it's sometimes well to handle them with kid gloves and discretion.

CHAPTER 14

The
Palm Beach Story

A car pulled to the side of the road. A door opened. A passenger was thrown out. The door slammed shut and the car sped away. One more abandoned puppy, one more statistic. Case closed as far as they were concerned.

He ran after the car. He ran until he couldn't run anymore, then he walked until he couldn't walk anymore. The puppy chased after the car for about a mile or so, then, completely exhausted, he sat down on the soft shoulder of the road. He wondered why they had left him behind and when they would come back for him.

The little guy was frightened and confused. He didn't know what to do or which way to turn. He looked up and down the road, but there was nothing. No trace of the car or his family. The only thing in sight was a large white house set behind a wall.

While he rested, catching his breath, the gates of the wall

opened. A big blue car with two small white dogs passed in front of him and turned left into the driveway of the white house.

The car disappeared as the gates slowly closed. Halfheartedly, he barked after the car, "Help me, I'm lost!" No one heard him.

His nose to the ground, the puppy started the mile back to the drop-off spot. He slowly retraced his steps. He wanted to get there, he wanted to be waiting for them when they returned. He was sure they would come back for him. This had to be a mistake. Reaching his destination at the mile's end, he nervously waited and hoped.

The day passed. No one came for him, no one showed up. He was getting hungry, he wanted something to eat. He was tired, he wanted to go home. But it seemed this was not to be. It slowly started to sink in. They didn't want him. They didn't care about him. They weren't coming back for him. He waited until he just couldn't wait any longer.

He walked slowly along the sand dunes overlooking the ocean. If he were now to disappear from the face of the earth, the only record that he had ever existed, the only visible evidence of his having been alive at all, the only markers of his sojourn, would be the trail of paw prints that he left behind as he moved on. Before long, the winds blew them away as well.

Our abandoned, frightened puppy hadn't been given much of a chance to make it in this world. In the dunes, he was just another speck of sand.

He was emotionally and physically drained from the day's traumatic experience. As the night came and having nowhere to go, he curled up into a ball and cried himself to sleep.

He dreamed about the highway, he dreamed about the white

house, he dreamed about the two white dogs in the big blue car. He dreamed about something to eat and a place to sleep.

Those who had abandoned him, he now abandoned. They had no place in his dreams, and no longer any place in his heart.

As the sun came up and touched the sleeping puppy, its rays caught him just right. For an instant he became a golden dog. The sun had done its part.

The flash of gold caught the wind's eye and interest, and it came in for a closer look. The wind wanted to make certain that a puppy really was there, sleeping in the sand. There was one. The wind was enchanted with the find, the buried treasure.

Mother Nature and her gang, the wind and the sun, decided to intervene in the fate of the golden, sleeping sojourner. To give a helping hand to the abandoned puppy. This innocent had suffered enough.

While sleeping, oblivious to what was happening around him, the sand-covered, golden puppy was about to have it all. This castaway had drawn some powerful friends into his corner. He had drawn them in with his puppy power.

The winds of serendipity would carry him to a new place, would carry him on a fantastic journey.

Fate, disguised as a brisk morning breeze, blew in from the ocean and across the highway. Its currents picked up a pamphlet that listed the most valuable homes in Palm Beach and sent the expensive real estate news sailing down the road, giving it no special consideration.

This pricey communication landed in the sand dunes. Before the wind could pick it back up, before it could climb out of the sand and ride again on the currents, continuing its flight, it was suddenly pounced on.

The journey of the upwardly mobile pamphlet was finished. This expensively made, full-color brochure was now under the forepaws of our puppy, the golden sojourner, a modern Odysseus.

His almond-shaped, hazel eyes curiously absorbed the contents. What was an A-list? What did *one-of-a-kind* mean? The PR jargon confused him, but he sure loved the pictures, though; the oceanfront mansions, the pastel palaces, they really caught his imagination.

One in particular stood out above the rest, a white palace with pink, terra-cotta, slate-topped towers. It looked familiar to him. He had seen this one before. Then it hit him. His ears went straight up in the air. This house was just down the road. It was the one where the two little white dogs lived. He stepped off the brochure and let the wind take it away.

Fate had done its job. It had given the puppy the pamphlet and an idea.

With the wind at his back and following the sun, Mother Nature's puppy took off down the highway.

The blue Mercedes 500 had traveled this road many times, South Ocean Boulevard, Highway A1A. Three were in the car. The driver, Catherine, was on her cell phone. She was wearing a little Westie dog on her left shoulder. This one, Katie, was looking straight ahead, maybe helping drive the big car.

The other dog, Jamie, another Westie dog, had her head out the passenger-side window, watching the world go by. Her small black nose vacuumed in every smell, nothing went undetected. Her ears listened for familiar and new sounds. Like a scientist accustomed to collecting data and assimilating it, she knew beyond any doubt that something new and different was in the air. The normal chemical makeup was off.

The puppy waited for the right moment. He blended in perfectly against the dunes; the driver wouldn't see him until he was ready to show his hand and make his move. And she didn't see him until she was almost on top of him.

What happened next, happened fast.

The Mercedes came rolling along doing about thirty miles per hour.

The puppy ran right out onto the highway.

Catherine saw him and hit her brakes.

Jamie and Katie were thrown to the floor.

Catherine threw open the door and ran out to see if she had hit the puppy. But he was gone, he wasn't there. He wasn't anywhere to be found. She looked on both sides of the road, trying to find him; maybe he had been hurt and needed help.

But there was no sign of the sandy puppy. Had she imagined this? Had he been a mirage? Had the sun been playing games with her? Relieved that she hadn't hit anything, Catherine got back into her car.

Katie and Jamie were excitedly barking and jumping around in the front seat. Catherine, thinking the two dogs' nervous excitement was due to the sudden stop she had made, didn't give it a second thought. She continued on home.

She pulled into her driveway, drove up to the front of the house, and cut the engine. She opened her door and got out of the car. Jamie and Katie followed as usual. Before Catherine had a chance to close the car door, the puppy made his appearance. He jumped over the back of the front seat, flew out of the car, ran up the steps into the house, and sat there. Tail wagging, head tilted to one side, ears up as far as he could get them, and eyes as wide as possible, he sat there, waiting and putting out maximum puppy power.

Catherine couldn't believe her eyes. Sure enough, there was A1A Sandy, as he would be known from then on. He was hungry, dirty, covered with sand, and full of hope.

Apparently, when Catherine had gotten out of the car and walked around the front to see if she had hit anything, the puppy had run around behind the car, jumped in the open door, and hid on the floor in the back.

This was one sandy puppy determined not to be left behind anymore.

Catherine did the only thing a person with a big heart could do. She adopted the kid. It was an easy adoption. There were no legal papers, no lawyers, no agencies to deal with. There was just a deep sigh and a final "You're in, kid."

Sandy smiled. You could've sworn he gave Jamie and Katie a wink, or maybe he just had a speck of sand in his eye. Maybe.

After being tubbed and scrubbed, a good, hot meal was in order.

The chef put out three bowls of a hearty conch chowder to start, followed by platters of large chunks of delicately spiced, grilled tuna with a side of string beans, carrots, and mashed potatoes. The dessert was a nice big piece of banana cream pie.

A1A Sandy looked his dinner over carefully. He watched the other two eat so as to get some idea of what to do and where to start with this strange, new food, this food with all its wonderful smells.

He didn't want to make any social faux pas in front of the girls. It took him ten seconds of staring and another ten seconds to wolf it all down and lick his platter clean. He also learned how to politely ask for more and more and more. It seemed in this house the food never stopped coming. Niiiice.

Fat and full, A1A Sandy went to bed. A giant bed that he shared with Jamie, Katie, Catherine, and her husband. Lying on his back, with his head tilted to one side, and a smile on his face, Sandy fell fast asleep.

Due to his whole reversal of fortune, A1A Sandy was now convinced that he could make a difference. He had dreamed a dream and it had all come true. He figured he could make things happen. He figured he must be a lucky dog. He would now dream another one, a real big one this time.

He would dream that all the many millions and millions of dogs and cats in the world could find what he had found. Good company, good food, lots of love and understanding. And above all, a good, safe place to sleep, and dream. In simple terms, the good life.

Would his dream come true? We're waiting to find out. After all, golden Sandy, like all animals, is Mother Nature's puppy. And nobody fools with Mother Nature's puppy, for long, and gets away with it.

Everyone is allowed to have a dream for a perfect world, even if the dreamer is a little dog.

A Hole in the Sole

She walked down the street with her boxer dog. She stopped. She wanted to show how "well trained and disciplined" he was. What a good dog he was. She snapped her fingers and he sat. She snapped her fingers again, and he lay down. Well, he almost did.

She said that the prong collar on his neck didn't hurt him, it had plastic tips. The nylon constraint around his face, even though it rubbed the bridge of his nose raw and twisted his head, she said was a "gentle-type controlling lead" and it didn't bother him at all. She said this face-puller was very humane.

The boxer had dry skin and sores. She said he was getting steroids for that and the drugs would take care of the problem. He was scratching himself raw. She said that was just dog stuff, just an itch, all dogs scratch an itch. She said he sleeps comfortably in his very own cage/crate/condo. She said he eats the best dry food that money can buy. Said she saw it advertised on TV.

Is this the relationship you always dreamed about? Where's the connection?

This is not a connection with an animal. This is the possession of something controlled by drugs, devices, and excuses.

No matter how you try to paint this picture in a nice, positive, caring light, it's just paint. It's not a van Gogh, it's a counterfeit. In this picture, the animal is paying the price.

Good intentions gone bad. Bad information leading to the possibility of a giveaway. Like a Sandy dog being thrown away like an old shoe with a hole in the sole. Where is the connection?

We love to have Mother Nature, Lady Luck, serendipity, the sun, the wind, and the moon on our side. But what it comes down to, in the final analysis, is you. It takes responsibility on your part to make certain that your animals are healthy, well cared for, and understood. You have to learn how to bring up your dog and cat the right way. Not somebody else's right way. But yours.

That comes in the light of truthful, straightforward, commonsense information and rides the winds of love, compassion, and understanding.

Taking a word out of Sandy's playbook, it takes good food, good company, and a good place to sleep.

Don't let the Soul Mirror become a hole in the sole of your shoe.

CHAPTER 15

Listening
for Plum

"Out of the tree of life I picked me a plum."

Plum was the name of my best friend, my pal. He was a purple-
gray weimaraner. So I nicknamed him Purple Plum, and then
as we got to know each other better, I called him just plain old
Purp.

Young blue eyes, Plum was born to an English mother and a
German father. He could have been related to the Hapsburgs,
as the Baron Von Langindorf once told me, or he might have
had a little bit of Brit royal heritage. But whatever the case may
be, it was his intelligence, personality, style, and good looks
that attracted me to him.

Plum was a pathfinder.

This nose dog, this feather and fur tracker was good. He
could smell out and track down my extra-cheese pizza with anchovies before I even picked up the phone to order one.

How did he know I wanted some pizza? Did he smell something in the air? Did he notice any subtle moves or mood changes in me? Did he read my mind or did he put the idea there when he felt like a slice with extra cheese and anchovies? I think he was capable of doing both. The next day, the "order" would be for Chinese dumplings.

His menu patterns were varied. He loved all the different foods of the world and planned his daily menu du jour. He always shared his food, after all, noblesse oblige. And he never argued with me when I paid the bill.

When Plum and I would attend dinners and parties, he had a habit of staying close to me. People were generally impressed by this, thinking Plum was a loyal dog. He was, but he had another agenda, a more ambitious one.

To him, I was also a great and steady food source since I had a talent for accidentally dropping food off my plate. Plum cleaned up after me, eating all the evidence as it landed on the floor. He kept my secret a secret. No one was ever the wiser, and we were always invited to social functions despite my social shortcoming.

His favorite restaurants were Peter Luger's in Brooklyn, La Grenouille, and P. J. Clarke's in Manhattan. Celebrities never have problems gaining access to these establishments, and Plum had become one.

He basked in a fair amount of fame and fortune did he, the purple Plum. But Plum was impervious to fame. He enjoyed making national television appearances, making movies and commercials, sure he did, but he was impervious to them as well. He took it all in stride. Nothing turned his head. To him, it was all just a day's work.

He took me with him to assist and always kept a sharp eye on me, making certain I didn't get carried away by the attention and get above myself.

Many tried to imitate Plum, but they were only pale imitations. They could never match his style, grace, talent, or shade of gray.

But with all the media attention lavished on him, he still preferred those lazy days in Central Park.

Up on a hill on Seventy-ninth Street and Fifth Avenue, right at the foot of a mulberry tree, he used to sit me down for hours. This was his favorite spot to talk things over, share ideas, and teach. He was always direct and to the point, never mincing or wasting words. He was never fooled by appearances, he could see through the veils of artifice and cut right to the quick.

Climbing the mulberry tree gave him a good vantage point to look out and see all. Over on Fifth, he watched the tearing down of a wonderful nineteenth-century mansion, and the popping up of a sun-and-view-blocking condo in its place.

Plum was always interested in progress, but progress should generally be for the better. The manse was nice looking. The condo was just tall. His cool eyes, now adult green, watched with sadness the passing of an era. The manse was now history. His eyes often changed color to match his moods. These eyes looked darkly at what took away the sun.

He had opinions. He didn't appreciate the mandated yearly reduction of the dog run at Seventy-ninth Street and Fifth Avenue. This was also progress of diminishing returns.

As public offices and politics changed, the run got smaller by half, then by half again. Until the dog run became so narrow that you would have to put your dog in at one end, run him to the other end, and then take him out and start over. The run became like a one-way lap pool, with dogs having to line up for their turn to get a little exercise.

He didn't appreciate the fact that whenever there was a lack of political causes to be championed, more restrictions would be put on dogs. Tickets for dogs off leashes, fines for noisy dogs, evictions for having dogs in apartments, and everywhere Plum looked he saw No Dogs Allowed.

One sunny, summer day when Plum and I were hanging out on the hill, I took my shirt off to get some sun. A police officer on a horse rode over and offered me a choice. Which ticket would you prefer? Do you want a ticket for indecent exposure or for a dog off leash? To tell you the truth, neither one sounded appealing, but I chose indecent exposure because I was young then and had a good body. Plum smiled and thanked me for not involving him in this crime of the day.

Plum was a great teacher. No, he was more than a teacher, he was my best friend. His connection was lasting. This able tracker, this influential mind reader, put me on the trail I've been following to this very day.

He died one winter. I had him cremated. I took his ashes, still warm, to the mulberry tree up on the hill, our favorite early-sixties hangout.

It was a cold, cold day. No matter what you wore, it just wasn't enough to keep warm. You could feel the cold right to your bones. It froze the spirits in your breath.

The ground was rock solid. It took me over an hour to dig a small hole. I couldn't see too well. I couldn't stop crying. My tears turned to ice as they rolled down my face.

I buried his ashes under his tree, the one he loved to climb. I missed him for a long time after he died, and I still miss him to this very day. I visit him regularly you see.

Plum. The memories keep coming back.

This great, gray ghost shadows my thoughts and keeps me honest. Still instructing and influencing my work, this silent observer follows me daily.

Once in a while, Plum comes in to consult on a case. We appreciate his expert opinions and advice. His truthfulness, tolerance, acceptance, and love are always helpful.

I can hear him, sometimes loud and clear and sometimes like a voice on the wind, silent but unmistakable. And I always find myself stopping to listen, listening for Plum.

You never lose those you love, not when you hear them, not when you listen for them.

I miss my friend. . . .

I sit by the tree, reach back, and touch the past. November 1998.

A thank-you to all of those who have been the closest to us, who have touched our lives and left a lasting impression. To those gone, but never forgotten.

List of honor:

Dukie. Tonto. Rebel. Plum. Sleepy Joe. Inches. Snapper Dan. Punker. Snowy. William. Minnie. Dinah. Piper. Mopsy. King. Candy. Lucky. Lady. Rocky. Magic. Saturday. Sunday. Taj. Misha. Pasta. Guela. Kasper the Grape. Sophie. Brady. Rip. Mollie. Lola. Sidney. Shane. Hippi. Cammie. Jake. Attila. Leroy. Ace. Beauty Lily. Tiger. JD. Jocko. Kelly. King. Whitey. Sunshine. Juniper. Razzle. Cinnamon. Whitney. Ninja. Gittle. Lance. Joey. Oscar. Nugget. Yussel. Steve. Dorrie. Zoie. Fluffy. Reggie. Emma. Tanka. Mr. Schaefer. Angus. Butter 1. Chablis. Wilhemina.